SANTA

All Customers Are Irrational

Understanding What They Think, What They Feel, and What Keeps Them Coming Back

William J. Cusick

AMACOM

American Management Association

New York • Atlanta • Brussels • Chicago • Mexico City
San Francisco • Shanghai • Tokyo • Toronto • Washington, D.C.

This publication is designed to provide accurate and authoritative information in regard to the subject matter covered. It is sold with the understanding that the publisher is not engaged in rendering legal, accounting, or other professional service. If legal advice or other expert assistance is required, the services of a competent professional person should be sought.

Library of Congress Cataloging-in-Publication Data

Cusick, William J.
    All customers are irrational : understanding what they think, what they feel, and what keeps them coming back / William J. Cusick.
        p. cm.
    ISBN 978-0-8144-1421-7
    1. Consumers.   2. Consumers—Attitudes.   I. Title.

HF5415.32.C87 2009
658.8'342—dc22

                            2009007651

Printing number
10 9 8 7 6 5 4 3 2 1

To my wife, Marti, for her patience and sense of humor, and to the crew at Vox, for making work fun.

Contents

Introduction

First, let me clear something up. We've all seen what we think are truly irrational customers. It's the guy at the front of the line at the fast food joint yelling at the teenager working the counter because he asked for no onions on his sandwich. Or the woman in the shoe store screaming at a wincing salesperson simply because the size she needs is not in stock.

That's not what we're talking about in this book.

While stories about crazy, zany customers are entertaining, they don't make for a particularly useful business book. They don't tell you how you can improve your own business. Instead, we're discussing *all* customers, including you and me, and how we all think about and act in the world around us. What we've learned over the last few years is that we are all, in fact, irrational. And irrational isn't all that bad. In fact, it could be the key to a better business for you.

Based on a wealth of research and some surprising new insights into how our brains work (and how they don't work), it's now clear that companies have been approaching customer service and retention the wrong way. Those who understand this and embrace new methods of attracting and keeping customers have an opportunity to create a game-changing customer relationship, one that could have an exponential impact on their profits.

While companies have traditionally taken a logical approach to gathering information about their customers, and have made "logical" assumptions about what their customers want and how they might act—and then have tried to fulfill those customer expectations—the reality is that customers don't really know what they want, and cannot predict (or tell you) what they will do anyway.

I'm a business person (I have a law degree too, but don't hold it against me). I help companies become more profitable. I do this by "showing them the light" regarding the value of their customer relationships and customer experience. For the last twenty-three years I've been involved, in some capacity, in customer experience issues, and through that experience I've seen the good, the bad, and the ugly in terms of how companies attract and manage their customers. One thing I've found is that, what many companies see as "best practice" regarding customer research, product design, service, and processes was more the result of custom or perhaps even ignorance, than insight. And that led me to move beyond the traditional business disciplines to more fundamental questions about how the brain works.

So in this book we'll look at recent research, and we'll delve into neuroscience and behavioral psychology. But, unlike some of the brilliant authors in this area of inquiry, such as Dan Ariely, Daniel Dennett, and Timothy Wilson, who are much smarter about these things, we're not going to focus on simply the idea of an irrational subconscious, or how we *really* absorb and process information. It's interesting stuff, to be sure, and I'm fascinated by it. But my concern is how these findings relate to your business generally and to your customer behavior specifically. How do you take this new information about how your customers think and transform your business research, products, services, and processes to maximize desired customer behavior?

There was a hot dog place in my hometown called Little Louie's. I'd stop there as I was biking home, sweaty and sluggish, from my summer job as a caddy at a local country club. Little Louie's sat, slouched really, next to the village green in the center of our suburban town, just north of Chicago. To grab a shake or a hot dog, you would open the squeaky wooden screen door and stand in the un-air-conditioned heat of the claustrophobic storefront. Little Louie's was always crowded, hot, and noisy. A group of anxious customers, jockeying for position in front of an old wooden counter, faced forward with mouths open and eyebrows up, trying to catch the attention of either Ed, one of the founders, or Louie himself. There was no line, but more of a mosh pit; it was up to you as the customer to compete with others to get noticed.

The walls were hidden under dozens of paper plates, each listing a scrawled, faded menu item–some still available, some not. Tacked among the paper plates were assorted autographed black-and-white photos of unknown vintage, many showing older Chicago sports figures like former Blackhawks, Cubs, and Bears, smiling with Ed or Louie.

"You!" The shout was always shocking. If you weren't paying attention, you could get passed over in a micro-second when Louie yelled and pointed at your gape-jawed, confused, 14-year-old carcass.

"Hot dog, no peppers, and a chocolate shake," I'd mumble.

"Speak up!" he'd scream over the din. I'd repeat, louder, a nervous adolescent squeak in my voice. Occasionally, you'd hear a first-timer, usually a guy in a suit, ask for ketchup on his dog, and the customers would all shut up and stare, waiting. "Ketchup?" Louie would start. "What are you talking about? You don't put ketchup on a hot dog!" (*Hint: When in the Chicago area, you traditionally don't put ketchup on a hot dog. Yellow mustard, a kind of neon green relish, and sweet and/or hot peppers, maybe some sauerkraut, though that's more for a Polish, but not ketchup.*)

Banging out the screen door toward the shade of the park across the street, sipping on my shake in its misbranded cup (Louie's never printed its own cups; they just bought overruns), grasping the crumbled plain brown bag with the dark grease stain spreading along the bottom (from the fries dumped inside, which you didn't order, you just got), I was a happy camper.

I loved that place, and so did a bunch of other folks. (In fact, there's even a Facebook group sharing memories of experiences at Little Louie's.) But why? Nothing about the experience I've described was in line with any traditional guidelines around a quality customer experience. They weren't particularly nice to their customers, they didn't appropriately brand their business, the food was a commodity. But there was something deeper, more emotional at work—something that's hard to put your finger on.

Compare that to another restaurant in Chicago my wife and I went to recently for a special anniversary dinner (I won't mention the name). The price of an entrée ran about twenty or thirty times the cost of a meal at Little Louie's. Chairs were held out in synchronized fashion for us as we sat down. The food was meticulous, strange, and delicious. Every time I took a sip of water out of my crystal goblet (we'd requested simple still water), two waitstaff would step forward from either side of the table, mirrors of each other, and formally fill our glasses from exotic-looking bottles. I pictured the waiters disappearing into the kitchen and walking over to an industrial sink to refill the bottles out of the faucet. For many friends, this restaurant, food, and service were the ultimate. Why was that? What is it that customers are really responding to? Did the water, sipped from expensive stemware, taste better than back home in your kitchen? Is it the product, the level of service? Certainly that's much of what keeps us all coming back to certain businesses. But there's more, and it has to do with how we think, and the power of our "irrational subconscious."

The truth is, we don't think the way we think we think. The prevailing wisdom had it that the subconscious handled some of our more primal processing, with just our most basic motives and fears lurking in the "subconscious, irrational" shadows, only to be accessed through various forms of psychotherapy. On the contrary, more recent research and studies show that the lion's share of our more sophisticated thinking and reasoning occurs at that deeper, so-called irrational subconscious level than previously assumed. Among other findings, research has shown that what we thought were conscious decisions and actions are, in fact, processed in the subconscious, with the small (5 percent) conscious portion of our brains often being notified after the decision has been made. Given that, the reasons we act the way we do are much less clear than some might assume. It can even be opaque to us.

The stakes in this effort have never been higher for you. A better understanding of how your irrational customers think can help you reshape how you do business regarding customer acquisition and retention. Every customer you keep has a powerful impact on your bottom line: Retaining a customer typically costs as little as one-tenth or less of the cost to acquire a customer. That translates into a significantly higher profit. Further, there is the surprising cumulative positive effect of keeping more of your customers. By bumping your retention up just slightly, you create a "compounding interest" for growing your customer base. In short, by increasing retention, you significantly reduce your marketing and sales costs while dramatically increasing overall profitability. Isn't it, then, worth the effort to better understand exactly how your customers perceive the world, process information, and behave?

Achieving that "irrational" connection with customers is the key to business success, and the answers lie within this fantastic puzzle box of our subconscious. And that's what this book is about.

Part
I

A New World:
The Economics and
Mechanics of Irrational
Customers

Chapter 1

The Bottom Line: Why Customer Experience Really Matters

Your customers are your only profit center.

Marshall Field

Given that we are all, on some level, irrational customers, throughout this book we'll be exploring how it's possible to create powerful, emotional, irrational experiences that drive key customer behaviors and, ultimately, profit.

But first, you might be asking yourself: Who cares? After all, companies have been profitable for decades—even centuries—by taking a business-like approach to delivering acceptable customer service and customer communications, if they have paid attention to customer experience at all. In fact, most companies have achieved success by focusing almost exclusively on customer acquisition, the hunt for the new customer. Year after year, budgets for marketing, advertising, and prospecting swell with the goal of increasing amorphous categories like "awareness" and "mindshare." Customer experience has been an afterthought.

But your customers can no longer be ignored! They're important. There are compelling social, technological, and economic reasons to pay more attention to how you design your customer research, processes, products, and communications.

It's no longer just about acquisition. The numbers, as we'll see in this chapter, bear this out. But more important, how you sell to, and interact with, your customers, has changed. That's because your customers—just like you—think and act in an emotional, irrational manner. Our brains are funny. We have odd ways of viewing the world. Context matters. Words matter. How you ask customers about their feelings matters. And whether you pay attention, and interact in ways that connect with that irrationality, matters.

It's Comcastic! How Times Have Changed

Stop me if you've heard this one: Several years ago, in November 2006, a Comcast technician arrived at a customer's apartment on a service call to replace the customer's modem. Apparently, the technician ran into a problem, and called into the Comcast service line. If you have any type of cable television or broadband computer connection, you've probably had a similar experience. It turns out the technician (being paid by Comcast) was put on hold (by Comcast) . . . for a long time.

At some point, the customer wandered in to his living room to find the technician sitting on his couch—phone to his ear, laptop open and leaning precariously on his knee, his head lolling back and a soft snoring noise emitting from his open mouth.

A few years ago, this would have resulted in one teed-off or amused customer (depending on one's personality), who may well have told a few people about his experience when the subject of cable or Internet connections arose. It would have been a negative incident for the company that had almost no repercussions, one lonely tree falling in a forest, with nobody around.

But times have changed. We are now living and working in a Web 2.0 world. So instead of shrugging it off, the customer quietly popped open his digital video recorder and filmed a few minutes of the inert, snoring Comcast technician. He then loaded it to his computer and added a few simple graphics explaining the context that he spliced in throughout the video:

> "A Comcast technician came to replace my cable
>   modem,"
> "He spent over an hour on hold with Comcast."
> "He fell asleep on my couch."
> (Then the customer got angry).
> "Thanks, Comcast . . ."
> ". . . for high prices"
> ". . . for three missed appointments"
> ". . . for promising to call back, and then not calling."
> "Thanks, Comcast, for everything."

Next, he posted the video on YouTube. You can still see it there, along with the thousands of comments from among its 1.2 million viewers (as of this writing). The popularity of the video made it a broader news story, appearing (or at least mentioned) on countless news broadcasts around the country.

What's really amazing is the shelf-life of this thorn in Comcast's side. As opposed to an angry letter, or even an item that appears on the evening news once, the video lives on. Even now, more than two years later, there are comments posted on YouTube every day. The majority of them relate primarily to other customers' frustrations with—and in some cases, hatred of—Comcast in all its different markets and manifestations.

Although the public relations damage to Comcast was significant, the company either had no reaction or whatever reaction it did have was undetectable. At the time, Comcast enjoyed a near-monopoly in many markets, at least for cable television service, and didn't appear overly concerned. Since then, however, as a result of more deregulation in the industry, competition has heated up, and customers have a choice of which cable, computer, and phone companies to do business with. The experience of Comcast customers now has a real and direct impact on the bottom line.

If you read what many customers have to say—not just on YouTube, but around the various virtual corners, watercoolers, and assorted other Internet forums where people gather to chat—it seems that Comcast is truly a poster child for poor, and sometime egregious, customer service.

So, do customers matter? I think you know the answer.

Are Companies Getting the Hint?

Even a company as seemingly indifferent to customer experience as Comcast is finally getting the message. It has recently asked several employees to leverage online Web 2.0 tools and forums like Twitter (the online "micro-blogging" social networking site) to monitor just what folks are saying about the company. Specifically, people like @comcastcares are now part of the discussion reaching out in real time to those who are complaining about specific service issues. The beauty is that the few Comcast people involved seem to have the power—or at least access within the labrynthine catacombs of Comcast's service structure—and the inclination to quickly help disgruntled customers get a resolution to an issue or problem.

This could be a dangerous move if seen by online users as disingenuous or simply a public relations ploy. But by all indications thus far (including my own observations on Twitter), they are engaging in real dialogues with customers and trying to help them solve problems. The company is just starting to dig itself out of a large hole in terms of public perception. It's safe to say that most consumers will not give Comcast the benefit of the doubt, given its track record. Still, overall it's a great move and could start rapidly building good will among a core group of Comcast customers.

But time will tell.

A New Dynamic: Customers Bite Back

I don't mean to be glib. It's always mattered whether your customers stay or leave, whether they buy more, what they say about your company. But there is now a new dynamic at play. The stakes have been raised when you treat your customers like second-class citizens; customers now have the very real ability to affect your profitability—not just by leaving, not just by telling their friends, but by tapping into the power of the media. Be it YouTube, Facebook, MySpace, Twitter, LinkedIn, Digg, or other online social networks, an individual customer can now—based on a single experience—influence the perceptions and actions of millions of other customers as well as potential customers. Add to that the electronic connection that most of us now utilize through instant and text messaging, allowing for real-time and viral spreading of both good or bad experiences as well as the connections between social and mass media (like CNN i-reports), and the stakes grow significantly.

Yet this is a customer environment that senior management at many companies has still failed to grasp. By understanding these social and technological factors, companies can take advantage of them, exploiting them in ways that enhance customer experience and perception. The future is, indeed, now. If you know you need to pay attention to these new dynamics, but don't know where to start, here's a suggestion: Stroll up to the desks of some of your twenty-something employees. As you approach, you'll see them close out their instant message conversation on their computer screen, minimize their Twitter screen, then hit "send" for the text message on their cell phone, put it down, take off their oversized earphones and hit "stop" on their i-pod, and look up expectantly at you.

They may have some ideas.

The Stunning Economics
of Customer Retention

Of course, it's not just the sea change over the last few years in terms of access to information for the average consumer, or the instant connection to others through the various social media, that presents serious consequences—positive and negative—for today's companies. Another aspect to consider is the sheer efficiency to be gained by devoting more resources and attention to your customer experience. The fact is that in most industries, any effort made to keep your best customers is exponentially more rewarding than your efforts to acquire new customers. How much more rewarding? In most industries, try three-, five-, even tenfold from a revenue and (more important) a profit standpoint.

The efficiencies are astonishing if you dig a little into the costs of acquiring a customer compared to working to simply keep a good one. For example, for every dollar you spend to keep a customer, you need to spend $5 to $10 to acquire a new one.[1] In banking, research has shown that it costs over $200 for the acquisition of a new customer; meanwhile many banks lose 30 percent or more of their overall customer base every year—customers who would, theoretically, cost one-tenth of that $200 to keep.[2] That's your choice: $20 or $200? It's even more pronounced in the cell phone industry. Acquisition costs top $300, and yet customer churn is rampant.[3] Even more egregious: For many of these industries, customers are typically unprofitable through the first year, only hitting a breakeven point later in the relationship (if they stay).[4] Yet these potentially valuable assets are walking out the door with little thought or effort put into retaining them.

The fact is that there is an exponential financial impact of focusing more on retention to drive growth. Yet companies still don't get it. Here's what I mean . . .

"Thank You, Sir. May I Have Another?"

Like many business people, I carry a Blackberry (no iPhone yet) around with me to stay in the loop by phone and email and, to some extent, instant and text messaging. (My employees and my wife sometimes get irritated when I shut it off so that I'm NOT connected, but that's a different book.) A few months ago, my Blackberry Pearl started going batty, screen flickering, track-ing ball inoperable, suddenly shutting off. I wandered into a T-Mobile cellular store and the employee helpfully pulled the battery out and put it back in. "Seriously?" I wondered. That's the solution? I had done this myself several times already, of course.

Several days and several store visits, software patches, and a new battery later, I was officially defeated. Striding to the counter I pronounced my device the sufferer of a terminal disease. A replacement was therefore required. The customer service employee—let's call him Biff to be clear it's a fictitious name—grimaced as he perused the screen of his computer. "Your warranty on this was up two weeks ago," he said, shaking his head and feigning sympathy.

I felt my ire rising. "So you can't replace it?" I asked. "We've been paying you guys a hefty monthly fee for this corporate account." This was true.

Biff shrugged. "You're going to have to buy a new one." He waved his hand, both dismissing me and indicating the assorted phones arrayed throughout the store. I wandered over to the newer version of my model (same phone, but now in different colors!). The tag stated a price of $99. I shrugged and moved back to the counter.

"I guess I'll go with the Blackberry Pearl," I said, pointing at the phone that was identical to the one I was throwing away, except in blue.

"That will be $349," Biff muttered.

I winced. "But," I stammered. "The tag says $99."

"That's if you are a new customer and sign up for a T-Mobile contract."

"But I already have a T-Mobile contract," I whimpered. "That's why I'm here and not at AT&T buying an Apple iPhone. Don't you see? I'm trapped."

Biff stared blankly at me. "The price would go down if you extend your contract."

I closed my eyes and tried to think of a happy place. "Let me get this straight. If I was just some Joe Smith wandering in off the street and signed up with T-Mobile, I would get the phone for $99. Since I'm a long-term customer, who has several people on a corporate account that's locked in for the next two years, and we've bought numerous phones from you, and the phone you sold me crapped out, I have to pay a premium price."

Biff shrugged and nodded. If he saw the irony, he wasn't letting on.

Of course, I really had no choice. I added a year to my contract to knock about a hundred bucks off the new Pearl price tag and went limping on my way, with my severely injured sense of justice and a conviction that someday I was going to tell a lot of people about my experience. I guess now I can check that off my list.

Like most cell phone companies, if T-Mobile would just do the math, they would realize that by pumping all of their significant marketing and promotion dollars into new customer acquisition, they are shooting their collective selves in the collective foot. Isn't it better, when you think about it, to spend a few dollars (say $30 to $40) to create a rewarding, emotional connection with a solid, profitable customer than to spend over five or even ten times that to lock down the next Joe who wanders in off the street?

Can You Hear Me Now?

By looking at the overall customer experience, and by devoting the time and resources to creating interactions that allow their current customers to feel some sense of investment on the part of the company in the relationship, T-Mobile could reap the economic benefits of devoted customers. Frankly, I'm amazed that more companies that are supposedly focused on the bottom line—like cell phone companies—haven't figured this out yet. If the choice is to spend heavily on customer acquisition while letting profitable customers walk, or to focus a fraction of that cost on keeping your best customers (while increasing profit and reducing overall costs), which would you choose?

This discussion has been taking place for years now in the European marketplace, where customer strategies (and the corresponding economic benefits) take center stage. For some reason, this period of enlightenment has yet to capture management's imagination in the United States.

Ammunition for an Increased Focus on Customer Experience . . . in a Marketing World

It's telling that you can find, in most companies, a director or VP of sales, a director of marketing or chief marketing officer, but rarely a chief customer experience officer with any real power. Yes, there are now more and more officers in companies that are in charge of "total experience" or "relationship management." But compared to the traditional sales and marketing functions, customer experience still maintains a second-banana status. Why?

Well, while some of it stems from a perception that customer experience isn't a real business issue, much of the problem is related to the traditional business hierarchy and to the "silo" effect (the distinct and segregated departmental divisions) across different business functions. If an employee is in charge of sales, there is a clean chain of command within that function. The VP of sales can determine and then initiate a certain plan or process through his or her line of influence. For true change or improvement in customer experience, the hierarchy is much more ambiguous. In general, there is less authority, given that many companies simply don't see the value. More important, however, to effect true customer experience improvement, you must cut across a variety of functions and chains of command. A comprehensive customer experience (C.E.) solution isn't comprised of just the obvious customer-facing interactions. Of course it includes product design and traditional customer service functions. But it's also impacted by call center policies, billing procedures, and by legal decisions and pricing. To build a truly transcendent customer experience, you must get commitment from all of these areas. You are forced to convince the turf owner in each of those different departments that it is beneficial to the company to make the changes, even if it might not result in specific benefits or credit for the individual department.

If you have ever been responsible for—or wished your company paid more attention to—the importance of improving customer relationships, you have probably also encountered the difficulty of championing real change, especially in a larger corporation.

When I worked at a major insurance company, in their home office in Northbrook, Illinois, I spent my last several years there running the customer communications area. We were responsible for writing and producing many of the communications—renewal packages and such—that were sent through the mail to the fourteen million or so households that carried auto or homeowners insurance across the country. The system that was used at the time was a classic example of old-school logistics and coordination.

Most of the mailings were customer letters and inserts that were preprinted and dropped into either bills or renewal packages. Millions of preprinted, generic communications were mechanically inserted at thousands per hour within the massive internal letter shop facility. The company would purchase paper by the train-car load and would bid out the thousands of print jobs that would be necessary over the course of a year to Chicago printers. The only major document that was generated with personalized information was called a declarations page, which basically laid out all the specific insurance coverage information, like limits and coverage term and that sort of thing. So basically, the customer received no truly relevant information, beyond the occasional "winterize your car for safety" generic topic.

Along with another employee, I thought there would be much for the company to gain by creating more personalized renewal communications, specifically laser printing the entire package for each customer, complete with a cover letter from his or her local insurance agent. We researched what it would take to make the conversion and began to campaign for the change. While we didn't have metrics to guarantee a certain financial return (I wasn't as smart as I am now), we made the best case we could, which amounted to "It's good for customers!" But nobody was interested.

Nobody was interested, that is, until we started calculating the amount of expense savings to the company were we to move over to this type of laser-generating system. The savings, mind you, had nothing to do with the immense benefit the company would see from a bump in customer retention due to a stronger relationship that could be built between a customer and the agent. (Just to give you a sense of the magnitude: A 2 percent increase in customer retention—that is, customers who choose to stay and renew their policies each six months—would result in hundreds of millions of dollars of additional income for the company).

No, the thing that got senior management's attention was the expense savings from reducing the processing costs (no more outside printers would be necessary, as everything could be generated in our in-house facilities), less paper wastage (no more throwing out preprinted customer forms and letters that had become obsolete), less need for procurement time and resources, and potentially less postage. The savings were around $27 million.

Yes, it was great to get the green light for this initiative, since we knew it would end up improving our customers' experience. And sure, $27 million is a lot of money. But for a company as large as this one, it was chump change. And consider this: Cutting expense might be a worthwhile exercise for a company, but research shows that by allocating resources to increase customer retention by just 2 percent (2 percent!) you can decrease your expenses by 10 percent![5]

This is a point that many, many companies miss. At the same time, the very best companies understand and embrace it. It not only makes good common sense, but great economical sense to spend the time and the money delving into who your customers are, which among them are your most profitable, and how they think, then doing everything you can to keep them.

"Real Growth": Tougher Than You Think

Many companies are missing the boat on a golden opportunity to turbocharge profits. Instead, they are increasing their costs with an inefficient approach to getting and keeping customers. Another way we talk about this with our own clients is a concept we call "Real Growth."

Imagine you are a marketing vice president for a large consumer company. It's almost the start of a new year and you've been told your growth goal is 12 percent. Sound reasonable? It might or might not be. Let's look more closely.

We'll assume your goal for this past year was 10 percent, which you hit. So you need to bump that up just a couple more points, from 10 percent to 12 percent, right?

But that's not right. Growth isn't just based on adding new customers to those your company already has. The first step should really be to look at your customer retention. How many of your customers that were here at the beginning of last year are still here now? Let's say you know that number is 85 percent. In other words, Out of 100 customers, 85 remain at the end of the year. Yet you grew your total number of customers by 10 percent, meaning you ended up with 110 customers.

So that means your actual growth rate was closer to 25 percent, not 10 percent. Twenty-five percent! That means marketing and sales are responsible for acquiring more than a third of the customers every year. At the very least, that indicates the marketing and sales directors' jobs are tougher than even they assumed. But it also points at some interesting conclusions about gaining and keeping your customers.

Let's expand the numbers into something more realistic. If a company has 100,000 customers at the beginning of the year, and 110,000 at the end of the year, the apparent growth rate, as we said, is 10 percent. Easy so far, right? So, if a company with a 75 percent retention rate (which is average in many industries) is growing at 10 percent, it really means that the company must be *acquiring an additional 35 percent new customers* during the year. And these new customers cost *five to ten times more* than it would cost to keep existing customers. Just imagine the exponential economic impact of increasing retention by just 5 percent.

How much easier would life be in your company if everyone understood the daunting challenge created when you place the emphasis on marketing and acquisition to achieve the organization's financial goals? How would life change for the marketing director if he or she was able to respond to the 10 percent goal by saying to senior management: "Do you realize you're really expecting me to grow by 35 percent?"

And what about the person (Is it you? Is it anyone?) who is "in charge" of customer experience and retention? What can you do if you're armed with this knowledge and can apply it in your company? Would it change how your company talked about and acted upon customer experience issues if you knew that you were five to ten times more efficient when you retained a good customer as opposed to grabbing a new, unknown one?

Finally, consider how, if you understand the concepts we will talk about in this book regarding how people think, your company can manage for this type of growth. And guess what? There are even more bottom-line reasons to work harder to retain your customers.

The Beauty of Compound Interest in Customer Retention

My son, Sean, is 17. He is your typical teenager: plays lacrosse at his public high school, grudgingly does his homework, tries to learn electric guitar, and likes to hang out with his friends on the weekend. Over the last few years, he's had a variety of methods for making money, including babysitting ("So easy," he says. "I just goof with the kids until like 8:00, when they go to bed, and then I watch TV") and working at the park district coaching preschoolers in a sports class. In the summer, in particular, he was able to generate some decent money.

To teach Sean about handling his money responsibly, we set up a bank account several years ago at the local community bank. Sean would regularly make deposits, keeping some cash for spending on movies, bowling, fast food, and such.

Surely, this would be a great way for Sean to see the value of letting his money work for him! If he just left the money alone, he could see the power of compounding interest in action. As the interest he accumulated was added to the existing principal balance, and then yet more interest earned, Sean would understand the beauty of saving . . . right?

Not so much.

Instead, like many teens (and let's face it, many of us) Sean enjoyed spending his money. Much of it disappeared at McDonalds, and Nick's, and Micky's, and a number of other local fast food establishments. He figured he was making more money each week through his assorted jobs and activities and would keep depositing those future earnings. So, he thought, why not tap that balance when he needed it? And really, who can blame him? He's not doing anything illegal (to my knowledge, anyway). The money was relatively easy to earn, and much easier to spend than to save.

In a way, that's exactly how many companies approach the acquisition and retention of their customers. When the marketplace environment is growing, it often seems that acquiring new customers is a snap. When you need more customers, you just invest a little more in marketing and turn the sales volume knob up. Meanwhile, customers are wandering out the back door, shaking their heads, never to return. But the company doesn't really notice: The total number of customers continues to increase, because there are more flowing in the front door than are exiting through the back.

But what if the market turns soft, or through technological or other advances, the nature of your products or services must change and you must adapt? Suddenly, you're faced with a problem. You must spend more and more time and money to acquire new customers. It's a huge challenge. But you could avoid much of this if you understood the beauty of compounding the "interest" of your customer base through increased retention. In essence, this is the cumulative, positive impact created by raising your retention at all.

Look at it this way: Let's say that you currently have a retention rate of 84 percent. Remember, that means for every 100 customers that were around at the beginning of the year, you now have 84 left. You have a slow leak of 16 percent of your customers each year. What if you put some of the focus back on your customers? Imagine that you could increase and then hold your retention rate to 89 percent, not a world-changing challenge. Just tweak your customer experience, your processes, and programs to entice 5 percent more of your customers to stay.

That would mean, in the second year, you have—obviously—5 percent more customers, on top of your current growth rate. Good, but not great. Then, the following year, you just maintain that 89 percent retention rate. Same with the next year. So, what's the big deal?

It's this: You are piling those additional 5 percent of customers in the second and third year on top of the 5 percent from the year before. Take a look at the cumulative effect of just an incremental increase in your retention numbers.

As you can see, in the first and second year the additional customers you retain begin to create a positive impact on the total number of customers. Keep in mind that the growth rate and the retention rate remain the same once you've bumped retention up from 80 percent to 84 percent. But look at the growing and dramatic differential in the number of customers through years four, five, and six.

When I travel around the country, speaking to industry groups and individual companies, I'm always amazed at how

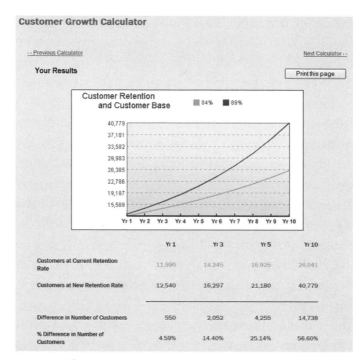

Source: www.voxinc.com

few organizations really understand (and more importantly, act on) this powerful business dynamic. Feel free to go to our website at www.voxinc.com, where we have a variety of customer retention calculators. Plug in your numbers and play with different scenarios. In minutes you'll have the ammunition you need to put a spotlight on your company's retention efforts.

Customer Profit: Marginally Speaking

We've already looked at some compelling reasons why customer experience really matters, and why you should focus your company's efforts on customer retention. I've got another one for you—one that's especially effective in industries where customer acquisition costs are high, and the goal is to achieve more than just an initial sale, such as insurance, phone service, or hotels. As we have already discussed above, it costs much less—as little as one-tenth as much—to keep a customer than it does to acquire a new customer. Also, as you've seen, by bumping retention up a few points and then maintaining that retention rate, you can take advantage of the beauty of cumulative growth of your customer base. Now let me enlighten you to one more interesting force at play regarding the bottom-line impact of improved customer retention, and that relates to individual customer profit margin.

In many industries (perhaps including yours) we know it costs a lot of money to attract a customer and convince him or her to sign on for your products or services. This is especially true in the financial services, where my company Vox does much of its work, but it's equally applicable in any industry where you are signing customers on for a series of interactions over time.

Let's look at insurance one more time to make this point. In the first year, as we've mentioned, it might cost over $300 to acquire a customer. The acquisition and servicing costs of that customer in that first year will typically outpace any corresponding revenue you derive. After all, you must add in the marketing and advertising (which might include direct mail and Internet marketing), the processing, underwriting, and inputting, and possibly agent commissions for the new customer. On top of that add any claims a customer might submit, and the whole affair is hugely unprofitable.

But consider that same customer in the third year of the relationship. The various marketing and other acquisition costs have long since been absorbed. Whether in insurance or another industry, the cost of simply servicing and maintaining the relationship is significantly lower. Yet the profit margin for this customer, who continues to pay the same amount (meaning your revenue from this customer has not changed from the first year to the third) continues to increase from one year to the next. In fact, it typically moves from a significantly negative margin in the first year to a highly profitable margin in the third or fourth year—all at the same revenue level.

If you know that you can put less money into a customer over the course of time and yet gain more profit dollars on that customer, why wouldn't you fight to keep him or her?

• • •

You are hopefully seeing the benefits to your business, in terms of the current marketplace, the efficiencies, and the sheer profit potential, of concentrating on retention of existing customers, at least in conjunction with the more general acquisition of new customers.

Ultimately, that's not at all what this book is about. Rather, we will be exploring some dimensions of how customers (and moreover, how everybody, including you and I) think. More specifically, we're going to examine some of the interesting aspects of how we all react in different situations to products, services, offers, processes, and communications. We'll identify how companies have "logically" approached these challenges. Then, more important, we'll explore just how your company can achieve a significant advantage over the competition by shaping these aspects of customer experience in ways that don't just increase customer retention, but also help drive other desired customer behavior, resulting in more cost-efficient service, higher revenue and—ideally—higher profitability.

We'll start by examining just what it means to be an "irrational" customer.

Chapter 2

Your Irrational Customers: A Look at How Our Brains Work (and Don't Work)

It has been said that man is a rational animal. All my life I have been searching for evidence which could support this.

Bertrand Russell

With any luck, I've convinced you that it's important—even critical—to better understand the impact your customers have on your company's bottom line. After all, customers are cheaper to keep than to acquire, long-term customers are typically more profitable than new customers, and a focus on retention can exponentially expand your customer base without any increase in your sales efforts. But, you might be wondering, now what? If you have the desire to push your company to a greater focus on customer experience, that's a good start. But you can't afford to fall into the trap that afflicts so many companies: implementing customer research, product design, and customer service based on old, ineffective management philosophies.

Our knowledge and assumptions about how our customers think and act have fundamentally changed over the past several years. And yet, most companies continue blindly down the old path. But not you! You can take advantage of this new knowledge to make substantive changes in your company's customer strategies. Let's look at just how differently our brains work from previous assumptions.

Irrational, But Not Crazy

We're all irrational. We have no choice in the matter. By "all," I mean you and me and each of your customers. You'll see that there is a delicate interplay between our logical but subservient conscious brain and our more powerful subconscious, or irrational, brain. It's this dynamic in how our brains operate that dictates how all of us, as customers, make choices and behave. By understanding those dynamics, we can then look at just how companies have traditionally approached disciplines such as customer research, product design, and customer service and consider some more effective methods for dealing with our irrational customers.

You don't need to become an expert in every technical nuance of how our brains work. While I've done some research into it, I'm certainly no expert in neurology or cognitive science. But the evidence that has been uncovered in these areas is too obvious and too important for us to ignore. It shines a light on our basic nature, and as businesses we can't afford to be oblivious, to march on using the same old approaches.

In order to create successful customer experiences and keep your customers, you won't be required to understand how the synapses and dendrites direct and fire electrical pulses, for example, and you won't have to gain intimate knowledge of the structure of the brain. However, with just a little extra information, you'll be able to gain some game-changing insights into how you can design new nontraditional research, products, and services to take advantage of the irrational way we all think.

The result can be higher retention and higher profits.

We Don't Think the Way We Think We Think

Over the last twenty years, it's become clear that how our brains work is fundamentally different than previously accepted. Neuroscientists, psychologists, and authors built on a progressive series of theories, experiments, and technologically enabled observations to paint a new picture of the brain. These findings and examples that have been impressively put forth by authors like Malcolm Gladwell, Dan Dennett, Gerald Zaltman, Timothy Wilson, and others. We will certainly *touch* on their findings as we discuss the particular quirks and idiosyncrasies that are a part of how all of us think and act, but the focus will be on how these pertain to your customers, and how companies have been missing the boat on how they research, attract, and keep those customers.

Let's start with some pure, observable science and move our way toward the really fascinating stuff. Take a moment, right now, to observe and feel your surroundings. What color are the walls or, if you are outside, can you feel a breeze in your hair? What does the air smell like? Are you sitting? Is the chair hard or soft? Is it easy to balance on the seat? Is your breathing easy or labored? When was the last time you consciously thought about your breathing? What about your heart rate? A moment ago, were you consciously thinking about any of these things? Probably not.

As you sit there, how many individual thoughts can you consciously hold on to? In the book *Strangers to Ourselves*,[1] author Timothy Wilson describes this dynamic, calling it the "adaptive subconscious." At any given moment, we are bombarded with 11 million bits of information. Everything from the temperature, to how your left pinky toe feels in your shoe, to that thing moving over to the side in your peripheral vision. And of those 11 million bits of information, you can consciously handle about forty at any given moment. Everything else is being handled by your irrational subconscious.

Let me repeat that: *Everything else* is being handled by your irrational subconscious.

Your heart rate, your breathing pattern, your balance, the spatial relationships of objects to your body as you move through a room . . . you don't need to consciously think about any of it. There is a powerful engine—your subconscious brain—that is working 24/7 to keep you safe and sound. Of course, you probably had some inkling that there was stuff going on under the surface in your day-to-day activities. After all, when you sleep, you keep breathing, right?

But this goes much deeper than some of the more automatic physiological systems that occur within your body. Much deeper and wider. So let's look more closely at this irrational subconscious.

This Is Your Brain, by Homer

For centuries, the assumption was that the majority of brain activity was conscious, while the subconscious was a dark, mysterious place, a place where Freud located our Id, a place that fueled our dreams and our darker motivations, but that had little to do with how we perceived the reality of the world around us or how we processed information and made choices. According to the philosopher Descartes, our emotional reactions are not just separate from our more logical, conscious mind, they are "opposing forces."

In fact, the truth is close to the exact opposite. We don't just deal with long-lost issues about our mothers or fear of water because of a childhood bathtub incident; rather, we process almost everything through our subconscious. According to Gerald Zaltman in his book *How Customers Think,*[2] a ridiculous 95 percent of all cognitive activity takes place in our irrational subconscious. I'm not strong in math (more right brained than left, I guess), but I figure that leaves a paltry 5 percent of your brain power occurring in our logical or conscious portion of the brain. And just what is that 5 percent of our rational brain spending its time on? It's not typically making decisions. Rather, it's rationalizing the decisions and actions we take *after the fact.* In other words, it's creating explanations and excuses for us as to why we behave the way we do.

To better understand just how the brain operates, let's take a look at an exemplar of truly irrational behavior, Homer Simpson, the lovable patriarch on the animated television show, *The Simpsons.* Our perception of Homer is that he is ruled by his Id, or his irrational subconscious. Here's what I project Homer's thought process to be in a typical situation. When Homer sees a pink frosted donut, Homer thinks (and utters, since there's apparently no filter between Homer's brain and his mouth), "hmmmm, donut." Then Homer starts salivating profusely, grabs the donut, and snarfs it down.

We like to think we are different in how we react to the world, that we are much more rational, more logical, even more noble. But in reality, we aren't too far from Homer. When you see a donut, you might picture the thought process this way: "That donut looks good . . . I know it's high in calories . . . and I'm trying to eat healthy and watch my weight . . . still, I didn't eat breakfast yet, so my calorie intake is low . . . and I'm really hungry . . . and it's over two hours until lunch . . . and so this is perfectly justified."

Yes, that might be what you "see" happening in your brain. The truth is most of that processing is happening after the fact. Your subconscious has already made the determination "eat the donut" and has instructed your hand to reach out and grab it off the plate. The reason you eat the donut? You'll never know. The determination occurred in your irrational subconscious, and all that back and forth ("reasoning," some might call it) takes place more or less in a vacuum, without access to the real processing that just occurred under the surface.

Irrational About More Than Donuts

For the most part, then, you, as well as all your customers, make choices and decide your next action without conscious knowledge. Crazy, yes? And this doesn't just happen with trivial matters, like whether to eat a donut. Almost every decision you make—from what to major in at college, to what car to purchase, to whom you might marry—is dramatically impacted by influences outside your immediate logical reasoning in a mysterious and, yes, irrational, yet incredibly powerful instrument called your subconscious.

Later in the book, we'll connect these influences to methods for leveraging the cognitive dynamics to shape your products, services, and experiences in ways that powerfully resonate with your customers. The goal is for the irrational subconscious of the customer to be a major consideration for you and your business as you shape new strategies, policies, and more in the future. For now, let's explore some more of this irrationality.

The Best Way to Make a Decision: Sleep on It

You might now be thinking that we are each wandering the Earth, making irrational choices that have nothing to do with logic. You would be wrong. The truth is that we're irrational for a reason. No matter what the choice might be, it's usually processed, in some capacity, in our irrational subconscious. And, as we will see here, that's a good thing.

Here's an example illustrating how we make better choices for complex decisions by letting our irrational subconscious loose and "going with our gut." In a recent experiment,[3] psychologists at the University of Amsterdam looked at a common but important situation: buying a new car. They randomly split participants into two groups and showed them both the same attributes of a new car. Then one group was given 4 minutes to consciously deliberate, weighing the positive and negative aspects to arrive at a decision. The other group was not allowed to deliberate. Instead, they spent the 4 minutes working on complex puzzles. The idea was to observe whether there was any significant difference in decision making between the group that consciously deliberated and the group that had to subconsciously process the information. Here's how it turned out: With just a few factors to consider (i.e., a "simple" decision), those who consciously weighed the few attributes did a little better, with 55 percent making the right decision, compared to 40 percent for the group who was distracted.

The experiment was then ratcheted up a level. Both groups were again asked to view positive and negative car attributes, but this time there were twelve instead of four. As before, one group consciously deliberated; the other was distracted with tests. And the surprising result: The success rate of those who consciously weighed the factors *dropped to 23 percent*; success in the "subconscious group" *shot up to nearly 60 percent*.

What's going on here? Most of us have been taught, from childhood, that it was important to be logical and rational when making choices. Consciously weigh all the important factors, then make an informed decision. But, as the test above and other research indicates, that's just not how things work. Yes, it's important to gather relevant information, but then it's just as important to let it stew in your subconscious. That's where the real thinking is going on. If we just try to analyze a problem in the rational part of our brain, the different factors and information don't help us, they distract us. We'll look at this more closely in Chapter 6.

The findings point to some time-honored advice when faced with a complex decision: "Sleep on it." Often, when we let our rational brains get in the way, we don't make smart choices. We're really neglecting the 95 percent of our cognitive processing power. Knowing this, can you already begin thinking about implications regarding how you deal with your customers?

The Power of Our Subconscious: Irrational-to-Emotional-to-Intelligent

If this is how people often make decisions on important choices in their lives, it seems obvious that companies must pay much more attention to this irrational thought process—perhaps even more so with expensive purchases.

Professor Antonio Damasio, in his book *Descartes' Error*,[4] suggested that, for any decision, there is only one question to be answered: "How will I feel if I do that?" The evidence suggests that it's emotion that ultimately drives a decision, and ultimately, customer behavior.

Just because it's emotions that may drive the decision, however, does not mean that the decision-making process is shallow. Damasio goes on to give an example, as outlined in the book, *The Advertised Mind*, by Erik Du Plessis.[5] If the choice for a customer is between purchasing a Porsche or sending a child to college, an emotional weighing of that question, "How will I feel if I do that?" would include considerations like the thrill of speeding down the road in a new car versus the guilt of preventing your son or daughter from furthering his or her education. Yes, it's a decision that requires logic, but at heart it's a choice rooted in deep emotion, and in the irrational subconscious.

What's that mean for your business? Consider another supposed logical decision, such as where you bank. If people really do make decisions based on emotions created in their irrational subconscious (and they do), then banks need to understand that those choices will be about more than the obvious, like the interest rate being offered on Certificate of Deposit (CD) products. Think of the opportunity for a bank that creates strategy around the irrational customer. It's critical that the question the bank is helping the customer answer is not just, "Who has the best products?" but rather, "If I decide to do business with this bank, how will I feel about that?" I hope you can see how making this fundamental shift in perspective can significantly change the approach a business might take to designing its customer experience.

The fact that our irrational subconscious is so primary to our actions isn't a bad thing; in many ways it allows us to deal effectively and efficiently with the world around us, as you see in the example above and will discover in other research and anecdotes we'll explore later. We'll also look at several studies and some recent scientific findings that demonstrate the remarkable way we are able to interact, make decisions, and more through the power of our irrational unconscious.

It's Evolutionary

Why are we set up this way? If we look at evolutionary theory, the quirky nature of our brains makes sense. As we developed, our survival as a species depended on our ability to quickly identify friend from foe. Our reactions—to run away or to stay and fight—had to be instantaneous in many situations. In *How Customers Think*, Gerald Zaltman provides an example: Think of walking down a path near your home, and you notice something long and slender on the ground near you. You jump away, even before taking the time to consciously process the information. Once you actually look at the object and take a breath, you realize it's simply an old garden hose lying on the ground. You jumped for nothing, right? Yet if it had been a poisonous snake, and if you had taken the time to carefully process the information before reacting, it could well have been too late.

This is our subconscious adding value in the most primitive sense. In essence, the irrational portion of our brain identifies patterns. Those patterns are either "good" or "bad." At its most basic, snake is "bad" because it represents a potential danger. As we've developed, it's natural to assume that this part of our brain has become more and more sophisticated. While we still subconsciously identify patterns, determining whether they are good or bad, the intricacy of these patterns is much more complex or subtle. In fact, as you move up, south to north, through the brain, the processing becomes more and more sophisticated, yet it's only the tip of this mental iceberg that we can consciously access.

How our brains got this way is an issue being researched and argued about right now. New techniques in neuroimaging and brain mapping have allowed unprecedented access to the brain's inner workings, and that has heated up the debate. In his entertaining book, *The Accidental Mind*,[6] author David Linden proposes that, far from the elegant miracle of nature others profess it to be, the brain is a bit of a mess. He contends that the way our brain works is inefficient, slow, sluggish, and far from perfect—the result of millennia of cobbled-together evolution. The miracle, really, is that, given its random, stuttering development, it works as well as it does.

Let Me Introduce You to Your Quirky, Unpredictable, Irrational Customers

Regardless of the nature of how our brains developed, there are aspects of how we think and act that have direct implications on how you need to approach your customers, how you communicate, how you design products, and more. Let's examine a few of the quirks that are a result of this somewhat random evolution. Call it an "irrational sampler." Then, throughout the book, we can look more closely at these aspects and examine how to take advantage of this knowledge to create compelling customer experiences that increase retention.

Customers Act Before They Consciously Make a Choice

Recent research has shown that people actually start acting before the rational or conscious mind is aware a decision has been made. This is the "Homer" phenomenon discussed earlier in this chapter. In other words, the irrational subconscious weighs the incoming information, makes a decision, directs the body to start moving in a certain way, and only then does it inform the rational part of the brain. In a way, when you make a decision and then act upon it, you are the last to know (at least consciously). This brings up some interesting questions about a customer's actions in relation to your company.

Customers Lie to Themselves

Seems silly, doesn't it? But it's the truth. Apparently, given that we often make decisions within the irrational, inaccessible part of the brain, and only then notify the conscious mind, it's up to the conscious portion to rationalize why we acted in the way we did. We infer what our feelings were, since we don't have access to the subconscious. In other words, we make stuff up. We're just guessing, telling ourselves stories. One might wonder, if customers can't access the "truth" about why they acted in a certain way, how companies get at the customers' true feelings. Good question. We'll look at customer research and just what it's worth.

Customers Can't Predict How They're Going to Act in the Future

If we're bad at accessing the irrational subconscious and telling ourselves the truth about why we act in a certain way, we're even worse at predicting how we might act in the future. Specifically, a customer, when asked how he or she might react to a future situation (like new features on a product or navigating through a redesigned website), is almost clueless. In fact, *other people* who know you are better at predicting your behavior than you are. Even people *who don't know you,* but are just told some things about you, are better at predicting your future behavior. Yikes! Just think about the implications for your company if you can't rely on what your customers say they want in the future. What can you do to stay ahead of the curve?

Customer Behavior Can Be Influenced by Almost Anything

From the design and colors on the walls of a room, to the temperature of a beverage you're holding, to the words you're exposed to, all have a major impact on your irrational subconscious, the emotions you generate, and in turn, your behavior. Studies (which we'll look at in Chapter 5) have shown that holding a warm cup of coffee can make someone behave in a more caring way than holding a cold beverage, or that reading words that are more aggressive can cause someone to behave in a less tolerant way minutes later. This influence over people's behavior is called *priming,* and we'll discuss it in more depth in later chapters. For now, think of your customers and your customer experience. Are they confronted with language, situations, or environments that might make them feel (and thus act) in a more positive or negative way?

Customers Think in Metaphors

We all do. In fact, our thoughts and our speech are littered with metaphors. Metaphors—pictures, logos, representative concepts—provide a direct conduit to a person's irrational subconscious. To take a simple example, consider advertising for one of the larger consulting companies. Does the company represent what it does by presenting complex business issues that it solves or in terms (visual and verbal) of "climbing mountains," "reaching the summit," etc.? Metaphors are like your broadband Internet connection in terms of effectively communicating fundamental ideas back and forth with your customers. Is your company interacting, talking, and presenting your brand, products, and services with that in mind?

Customers Apply Human Characteristics to Inanimate Objects

Take a look at your cell phone, your water bottle, or your coffee maker. One of our evolutionary survival traits, among other factors, is that we are hard wired to seek out and recognize human characteristics within these and other products. It's called *anthropomorphism*, and it's a powerful force. Anthropomorphic characteristics could include the look, feel, or capabilities of the products and help create a stronger, more emotional connection with customers. Dare you design another product without this knowledge?

Customers Want Products with Every Feature, But Then Don't Use Most of Them

Because, as I mentioned above, we are not very good at predicting how we'll behave in the future, when asked, we think we want all the bells and whistles on our new phone, watch, or coffee maker. But in reality, when it comes down to it, we just want to talk, check the time, or make a cup of joe. How do you balance your product designs to walk the line between being "the next big thing," and creating something that's actually comfortable and useful?

Customers Tell Themselves Stories

All of us have a primal need to make sense of our lives. Why did I do what I did in the past? Why do I stay friends with that guy or do business with that company? What kind of person am I? To do that, we connect up the big jumble of experiences, lessons, and people into a cohesive story—a story we are constantly, within our subconscious, amending and editing. As we each create our own narrative, it's an opportunity for companies to fit into those life stories.

Are You Up to the Challenge?

Your customers are just like you—irrational! If, as stated above, we don't think the way we think we think, it's time to look at the assumptions we all make in our businesses—assumptions based on something as simple as "that's how we've always done it."

But if you make these assumptions, if you go through the motions regarding how you conduct research, design products and services, and communicate with your customers, you're missing the boat. You have a tremendous opportunity that could transform not simply your customer experience, but your business itself.

Plus, there's one other reason it's worth the effort to reevaluate the way you are dealing with your customers. Beyond the improved retention, the lower acquisition costs, and the healthier bottom line, you actually have a chance to make your customers' lives a little better. There's a lot to be said for that, isn't there?

Are you willing to take the challenge?

Part
II

A Fresh Approach:
Strategies and Tactics for Keeping Your Irrational Customers

Chapter 3

Brand Promises: Who or What Are You, Metaphorically Speaking?

Key metaphors help determine what and how we perceive and how we think about our perceptions.

M.H. Abrams

Do you own a PC, or are you one of those Mac people? Personally, I'm pecking away at this moment on a cookie-cutter Dell laptop (that would be a PC) on Microsoft Word, which runs on Microsoft's Windows platform. It's relatively dependable—not very exciting, but it does what it's supposed to do for the most part, and it easily communicates with the other PCs in the office through our network.

Of course, I know other folks with Apples. You know some too, no doubt (or maybe you *are* one of "them"). I actually picture myself as more like a Mac person than a PC person. Do you know what I mean when I say Mac person? You've probably seen the Apple ads over the last few years, with the two characters Mac and PC. Mac is younger, hipper, more casual, and relaxed. He's also, according to the ad, brighter and more competent. PC, on the other hand, is dressed in an uncomfortable-looking suit, he's older, and more anxious, apparently for good reason. He has a serious streak of insecurity and is constantly trying—unsuccessfully—to best Mac.

These ads resonate with viewers, and when we look a little more closely, there's a solid irrational basis for why these spots are so effective . . . and also some food for thought as to how you develop, communicate, and "live" your own brand.

As we've already discussed, the predominant thought process in each of us resides in the subconscious or irrational recesses, in the area of the brain that generates our most powerful ideas and impressions, the area that dictates how we feel and act. It stands to reason. After all, as we've discussed earlier, research shows that 95 percent of our thought processes take place in the irrational, emotional subconscious. In other words, we think (whether we know it or not) through our emotions.

It is in this irrational landscape, then, that successful companies somehow must attain a solid footing. The companies that win in the marketplace do so, on the whole, by creating a brand or identity that establishes and then builds upon an emotional or irrational impression. It's not rational, and that's good; instead, it's about how the brand makes us feel. But if that's the goal, the question in developing such a brand is "How?"

Picture This: Using Metaphors

One of the interesting lessons to be gleaned from the explosion of neuroscience research over the last fifteen years is the discovery of just how central a role metaphor plays in how all of us take in, process, store, and communicate ideas. From a business perspective, metaphors can allow a much deeper, even sub-conscious, emotional connection between your company and your customers.

In short, at our deepest and most fundamental, we think in images. However, given our irrational, emotional brains, we aren't always aware of it. The distinction is effectively raised by Gerald Zaltman in *How Customers Think* when he says, "An important difference exists between *how a thought occurs* (neural activity) and *how we consciously experience a thought*, if at all, once it occurs." And much of "how a thought occurs," most research indicates, is as images. Further, Zaltman goes on, while the stimuli we receive include all five senses—sight, sound, touch, taste, and smell—what those different experiences or inputs trigger is an image of some sort. So, for instance, if you hear a snippet of a particular song (let's say The Clash's "London Calling"), it might evoke a sudden image of your younger self in the backyard of a long-ago friend's house party the week when you were graduating from high school. At least it does for me.

So, while we all use language to communicate with each other, and to some extent "consciously experience a thought," the emotional, irrational subconscious processing that we do— the thinking that really drives our behavior—is image based. And that is where the use of metaphor becomes so important to understanding how your company is being perceived, as well as to designing how to present the company brand.

Before I get too deep into this topic, let me define what I mean by metaphor. According to Webster's, it means "a word or phrase literally denoting one kind of object or idea is used in place of another . . ." That may be overly simplistic, but it serves our purposes. In particular, I'd like to explore metaphor as visual representations of ideas and brands.

In its simplest form, then, it's a way of saying that "this" is "that." For example, my *day* was a real *bear*. On the *road of life* it's important that you don't *burn bridges*. When *shooting hoops*, I was *on fire*. You get the idea. And while at first blush this might seem like a simple rhetorical device, the use of metaphors runs much deeper. According to Zaltman, the typical person peppers six metaphors per minute in his or her spoken language. It's core to how our brains work.

Let's look back at our example of Mac versus PC. Obviously, Apple is a large, global public corporation, with thousands of diverse employees of all stripes. And yet, through some research and clever advertising copywriters, Apple was able to land on the perfect (some might even say obvious) metaphorical representation of the company . . . or, rather, on the public's existing metaphorical perception of the company, that of "Mac" to Microsoft's "PC." In a way, that representation, through the hip, young, casual creative type of person, is the "anti-Microsoft." And that's an important point. They weren't making up the metaphor of how you should see Apple. They were simply tapping into the metaphor that already existed in the consumer's head, created over years through Apple's successful positioning of its brand.

The power in the ads, of course, lies in the dramatic contrast between hip Mac and old-school (and, frankly, kind of lame) PC. By personifying Apple, and then doing the same with Microsoft, the ads reach down to a deeper emotional core. Instead of saying, "Apple computers and software are designed to be very intuitive, with the goal of allowing users to accomplish a variety of tasks in an almost effortless manner . . . oh, and we're cooler than some other companies we care not to mention," the ads communicate that message visually through metaphor. And this sinks into our subconscious, making powerful impressions and connections.

In the past, advertisers have leveraged metaphor in two distinct ways. First, a company could use customer research to acquire insight into a customer's view of the company. It could, for instance, conduct focus groups to understand how customers picture them. This allows the company to gain some sense of customer perceptions regarding its qualities and values, without requiring customers to simply make their best guesses as to those qualities and values. There are several methods for digging into this issue, one from Zaltman called the *metaphor elicitation process*, with some techniques more effective than others.

The other side of the metaphorical coin, regarding how companies utilize metaphors, relates to how companies present themselves to the marketplace in a particular light. In other words, it's using metaphors as a communication strategy, as opposed to a research tool. That's exactly what Apple is doing in its broadcast ads with Mac and PC. But almost every company uses metaphor in some way, even if not as sophisticated. Think about your own organization. Do you have a logo? Isn't that just an image that represents something more? By designing a logo and dropping it into your stationery, business cards, website, etc., you are trying to establish a brand anchor in the minds of prospects and customers. The logo isn't your company; rather, it's an image or metaphor that makes people think of your company. Whether, when a person sees your logo, it evokes positive or negative emotions in his or her irrational subconscious is a question you may need to answer.

No matter your company's current situation, metaphor deserves a special focus when discussing your brand. If, in fact, we think metaphorically (i.e., thinking of "this" as "that," especially in images), wouldn't you want to spend some time exploring your company's identity in the same way?

What's *Your* Brand Promise?

At Vox, we participate in a variety of different customer-related projects and initiatives. We might be asked to help improve the online customer experience or to review the entire customer landscape—all the interactions and communications a company might have with a customer—in order to recommend a course of action to improve customer perception. But no matter the category of project, at the beginning of our discovery phase we always ask the client one question to get things started: "What is your brand promise?"

To be clear, when I say, "brand promise," I'm not asking about positioning, which is more a strategic discussion, wherein you map out the market position of your competitors and con-template how you can carve out a position or spot in the market and in your prospect's mind. Determining your positioning is a key discussion in your company, but it is more cut and dried; it is purely a business consideration. Brand promise moves to a different, more emotional level. Positioning is really about pure strategy. Brand promise is about an appeal to the customer.

We feel it's absolutely critical to understand what it is that this particular company is promising to prospective and exist-ing customers. What, in other words, are the customers' ex-pectations when they "buy" (whatever that might mean)? What is the distinctive value proposition? Some might even describe it as the company's soul. Surely a company that generates bil-lions of dollars in revenues each year begins all new work and initiatives from a common, consistent, and unique brand prom-ise—a *raison d'etre*, if you will—right?

Actually, not so much.

"The Question," as we call it, is almost always followed a by an interesting, albeit uncomfortable, moment—the preg-nant pause as the question flops about on the table, a couple of

nervous snickers, and furtive glances at the boss, the other attendees afraid to venture a guess for fear of unveiling their ignorance. After a minute or more of hemming and hawing, we'll
get a response like, "Uh, what exactly are you looking for when
you say brand promise?" Or, just as often: "Well, we're a, uh,
high-quality (or 'world class' or 'industry-leading'), low-price
(or 'efficient' or 'quick to market') global service provider (or
manufacturer or distributor)." Other attempts at articulating a
brand promise typically devolve into a several-paragraph-long
dissertation regarding the company's goals and mission.

And, of course, there lies the problem. When the senior
management team of a large organization is simply incapable of
articulating what it is that, at its essence, the organization does
for its customers, it means there is no starting point. And even
if the C-level executive group "gets it" and can easily state the
company's compelling brand promise, the message typically de-
teriorates as we move to the next management layer. Most often, by the time we're talking with front-line employees, the
concept of "brand promise"—if it existed at all in the upper
echelons of the company—has completely disappeared.

When we begin an engagement with a client that has no
satisfactory answer to our question, it makes our job extremely
difficult. Without a unified, distilled brand promise, there is no
anchor, no foundation. Whether dealing with issues concerning the company's promotion of a product or service, prospecting for new customers, customer communications, or customer
service, there is no common starting point. So, if there is no
senior management consensus on exactly what the company's
brand promise is to its customers, we try to help them come up
with something. Something is better than nothing.

Apple, it seems, wears its brand on its sleeve. That brand—
the mantra under which it operates and the unique value it
promises—can be articulated as: "Technology for humans."

Just What Is a "Brand Promise" Anyway?

No doubt you hear a variety of terms like *brand*, *brand promise*, and *positioning* as you discuss your company's image. It can get confusing, and not just for you. Part of the problem is that many of the practitioners in this arena use these terms in different ways, so let's make sure we're at least using them consistently in this book.

- *Brand*—In short, your "brand" is more a result than an intention. It's the perception your company has created in the minds of prospective or current customers as to who your company is and what it stands for.

- *Brand Promise*—Some call this brand essence. The brand promise is about company intention (as opposed to results, which is how the ultimate brand is measured through market research). It's really the distillation of what makes you distinctive as a company, and what expectations you are creating for your customers. An example would be Volvo, which could be described in just one word: safety.

- *Positioning*—This, as we briefly discussed earlier in the chapter, refers to the "space" your brand occupies in relation to other brands in the same category (for example, Tide versus Gain laundry detergents). Positioning is about defining a space within a market, by either bumping up against other players in the market (like Apple does with Microsoft) or through leveraging another brand altogether like saying you are the "McDonalds" of Indian food (i.e., your service is fast, the restaurants are clean, and the food is the same from one location to the next).

And that philosophy manifests itself through all aspects of the business. You not only see it in the ads, but in its commitment to its customers (or "fans," "devotees," "evangelists," or whatever you want to call them), their commitment to intuitive usability of its hip products, even the fonts on its documentation. The advertising all displays a commitment to being personal, cool, and connecting in a human way with users.

Microsoft, on the other hand, seemed to rely on the concept of "ubiquity" over "uniqueness." But ubiquity isn't a brand promise. It's a business strategy. Instead of identifying itself as a specific idea (or cause) to a particular group of people, it was "everything to everyone," the result of a licensing strategy that placed Microsoft operating software in the vast majority of the personal computers sold in the United States. As a consumer, you didn't really seek out Microsoft products; more often than not you simply felt you had no other choice. In fact, in doing a bit of research to help determine exactly what Microsoft's brand promise is, I came up largely empty-handed. The message seems to change over the years, and schizophrenia does not contribute to the success of a company. No consistency leads to no long-term brand equity.

Of course, one might argue that Microsoft is the winner here in terms of market share, capitalization, etc. But the game isn't over, and with the success of Apple's iPod and iPhone product lines, as well as inroads in personal computers and software, time will tell who, if either, (did somebody say "Google?"), will take a commanding share of the market.

Starting at Square One

It doesn't matter what size the company; this slippery concept of brand promise is a problem that many organizations don't even know they have. But it is, indeed, a big problem. At Vox we see a brand promise as a requirement—Square One, before any communications or other business efforts can take place. The challenge that we see with many of our clients is that they mistake a recitation of benefits, or worse, services, as a brand promise. But they are missing the point.

The brand promise must reach deeper down, into emotional, and yes, irrational territory. A brand promise must drive a consistent message . . . no, more than that: a commitment, which can nestle into a spot in the subconscious of your potential customer. It must be real and it must be sincere. In other words, it must be a promise on which you are able to follow through.

So . . . What Are You?

As we've seen, customers think in images. They feel and act based on what images are evoked based on your company's communications and interactions—both intentional and unintentional. So to ask customers to simply, on a logical, conscious level, articulate whether they "like" or "dislike" your company, and to give you rational reasons for their feelings, puts them in an impossible situation. We use words and language to interpret our deeper, more irrational (and yet more compelling) thoughts and feelings, and as I'll discuss in subsequent chapters, we're not very good at it. Better to ask the customers to dig as best they can and provide you with the image of your company, which in turn gives you clues as to how your brand is perceived that are closer to the truth.

So, one of the exercises we often employ with our clients is attempting to get at the real brand promise through metaphor. It's a method that has been employed in advertising in the past and it's akin to the PC versus Mac concept. The idea is to get clients to picture their company as if it were a person (some have used animals as well), tapping into the subconscious and irrational anchors for how they would perceive their organization.

What would this person look like? What type of attitude would she display? Would he be wearing a suit or a T-shirt? Would she be wearing jewelry? Is he confident, polished, urban, small-town? Is she sincere, fun, charitable? The idea here is not to *create* the personification of your company but to attempt to *define* what it really is at this point in time.

The Man in the Suit, or the Guy Next Door?

As an example, let's look at two companies in the insurance industry—Allstate and State Farm. There are similarities: Both are large, traditional, property and casualty insurance companies selling, among other things, automobile and homeowners insurance. Both are located in the Midwest and sell their products through exclusive agents and independent agents, as well as direct over the phone and online. There are also some differences. State Farm is a mutual company, owned by its policyholders, while Allstate is a public corporation, answerable to its stockholders for its results each financial quarter. But if you ask a group of consumers to personify these two companies, there's a good chance you'd end up with two very different pictures. The person we'll call "Allstate" might be a white male, dressed in a conservative blue suit, very professional and corporate in appearance. The person we'll call "State Farm," on the other hand, might still be a white male, but would most likely be more casual in appearance and perhaps be in short sleeves and wearing khakis and a tweed sport coat. "State Farm" would more likely be a smaller town resident, more likely to coach in the local Little League, and more likely to be a member of the Rotary.

Neither the image of Allstate or State Farm that customers or prospects might paint is necessarily good or bad. They are what they are: the result of countless exposures, news reports, customer communications, personal interactions, and stories from friends that build toward a universal impression. In your business, this personification exercise serves to paint a picture with customers or prospective customers of "who" they are right now, as a company. From there you must follow several more steps down the path to get to their real and valuable brand promise.

Be Careful What You Promise— Expectations Are Everything

It's no secret that the airline industry is in trouble. Skyrocketing costs to do business have resulted in increased ticket prices, fewer seats due to fewer flights that are inevitably packed, smaller seats, luggage surcharges, fuel surcharges, and elimination of free snacks. Clearly, it's going to be an uphill battle for airlines to survive.

That customers are unhappy in general with their treatment within the airline industry was highlighted in a recent satisfaction survey and ranking by the University of Michigan.[1]

(Note to reader: In the next chapter, I'm going to pretty well trash the notion of "customer satisfaction" as a meaningful performance metric within your organization. While satisfaction is a relatively weak predictor of future behavior under the best of circumstances, in this case it does serve to spotlight customer perception of one airline relative to another.)

The rankings indicated that satisfaction was down for almost all airlines, and for some they were totally in the dumper. However, Southwest Airlines came out, once again, at the top of the heap. In fact, Southwest ranked number one for the fifteenth straight time in this survey.

What, one might ask, is Southwest's brand promise? Unlike most airlines, Southwest doesn't make it a point in its advertisements to tell you about how comfortable its seats are or how attentive or luxurious its service is. In fact, it doesn't even offer you an assigned seat. Furthermore, when you arrive at your destination, attendants ask you to help clean up after yourself so that they can turn the flight around more quickly. Yet year after year, Southwest continues to rank higher in customer satisfaction than the more expensive, more "prestigious" airlines. Why?

Expectations Determine Customer Satisfaction

The answer lies in a strong irrational dynamic at play concerning the concept expectations versus satisfaction. It states that all of us possess a tendency to be very happy if our expectations for a certain type of experience are met, which makes sense. An example used by Chris Denove and James D. Power IV in their book, *Satisfaction: How Every Great Company Listens to the Voice of the Customer*,[2] is apt: If you are strolling into the lobby of the Four Seasons for a stay, you might very well have a "Louis Vuitton suitcase" of expectations. If, in turn, some small thing goes wrong—let's say a piece of toast is burnt—and yet the rest of your visit is to your standards (fresh flowers in your room, personal service from the concierge, pillow menu, etc.), you may be dissatisfied with your experience.

Let's look at the other side of the example: I was staying at a Hampton Inn in Birmingham, Alabama. In the morning, after a noneventful night, I was preparing for an important 9:30 meeting with the senior management team of our client, an insurance company, and I realized with sudden dread that I had forgotten to bring any neckties. Now, maybe at the Four Seasons or Ritz-Carlton in Chicago one could expect to phone down to the desk and have a smiling employee run up in with a variety of ties to choose from. But this was at 8:45 in the outskirts of Birmingham at a Hampton Inn. There were no stores to speak of nearby, and I didn't have a rental car. I walked down to the front desk to inquire as to any miraculous solution to my problem. The desk clerk called a co-worker, who ran outside and a minute later pulled the hotel shuttle van up to the door. He then sped me to an outdoor mall about four miles down the road that included a Men's Wearhouse. Even though they weren't open yet, I talked my way in and grabbed two ties off the table, barely looking at the prices. When the hotel employee dropped me back at the hotel with time to spare, it was all I could do to get him to accept a tip. He seemed genuinely happy that he was able to help me.

To say I was satisfied with the Hampton Inn in Birmingham doesn't do the experience justice. I was delighted.

The lesson for companies is to remember that customers naturally process their experiences based in large part on their preconceived expectations—expectations set in large part by the brand promise—of that experience. And if the experience falls short of the expectation, even if by a seemingly trivial amount, we can be disappointed.

Southwest started as a little regional airline in Texas. The story has been told countless times in the media, and in books like *Nuts: Southwest Airlines' Crazy Recipe for Business and Personal Success*, by Kevin and Jackie Freiberg,[3] so I won't bore you with the evolution of the company, although it's a fascinating study. The point is that, at the very beginning, Herb Kelleher, its president, stated the company's brand promise by advertising: "Southwest Airlines—The Low-Fare Airline." That was it. Yes, Southwest had fun and did crazy things in its marketing efforts (like dressing flight attendants in hot pants), but all of its business decisions were based on presenting the company as "The Low-Fare Airline." By setting its standard on one core idea—an idea it is able to live up to everyday—Southwest meets, and often exceeds, customers' expectations.

If we examine this a bit more deeply, there are some interesting implications. For instance, if a restaurant located in the Midwest professes to serve "the best filet mignon you will ever taste, period," the expectation is, needless to say, high for the restaurant patron *vis-à-vis* the filet mignon. If the filet mignon is marginal, the customer will, of course, be disappointed. But what if the filet mignon is above average, or perhaps even very good? The average patron might be satisfied. However, there may be customers who are used to dining at the Michelin-rated best restaurants in Europe who would be sorely disappointed in the restaurant, marking "mostly dissatisfied" on a survey. It would be better, perhaps, if the brand promise of the restaurant was "best filet mignon in the Midwest."

Or consider my original example, in the Introduction to this book: Little Louie's. What, would you guess, was Little Louie's brand promise? I'm not sure Louie could articulate it at the time (as a 14-year-old I wasn't thinking about it), but based on all outward appearances, there was no brand promise, beyond "hot dogs." In fact, it was almost the lack of a brand that was its most prominent feature.

And yet, really, I would argue that there was a brand, and it was infused in everything Little Louie's did. From the old, hot storefront in which it was located, to the greasy fries spilled into the bottom of a plain brown bag, to the misbranded drink cups, and finally to the caustic—but often humorous—interactions between customers and Ed and Louie behind the counter, Little Louie's brand was authenticity. It was real— what you saw was what you got—and that was what distinguished it from its competition.

Let's take another look at Southwest and the airline industry. What are some of the other brand promises put forth by the other airlines? Some, like American and United ("fly the friendly skies" doesn't really resonate these days, does it?), seemed to oscillate over the course of just a year or two, bragging about "more leg room," even changing the seating configurations within many of their planes. It was not long before they were moving the other way again, trying to generate more money per flight by squeezing a larger number of seats—and customers—onto each flight. What happened to their brand promise? Any idea?

Finding "the Nugget"

No matter the method or processes you use, the key to creating a really successful brand promise and its proper positioning is based on what we call "finding the nugget." The "nugget" is that one thing, a trait or belief, an attribute or philosophy, that is core to your company. It is that thing that separates your company from the others in your industry. But that thing needs to be real and significant; it must be something more concrete than "the best car" (why?) or "the cheaper phone service," unless, like with Southwest, you are willing to take the promise to the *n*th degree.

In the movie *Elf* from a few years ago, Will Ferrell plays a misguided, very large Santa's helper, who finds himself in New York City for the first time. He sees a sign in a diner window that says, "World's Best Coffee," and walks into the dank, depressing storefront to congratulate them on their achievement. The "promise" of world's best coffee in that case, of course, is silly to the point of ridiculous, but it's the type of mistake many companies make. The nugget you find must be real in order for it to be infused throughout your organization.

For us at Vox, that critical, core attribute or belief revolves around the concept of empathy. It's an emotional investment for each of us, and it centers in the commitment to understand the perspective of the customer, or the prospective customer. Internally, we talk about "walking in the customer's shoes." It's not just a methodology but rather a primary approach to everything we do. It comes through in our marketing, in our engagement processes, and in how we interact with and reward our employees. We even developed a proprietary service, called the Customerspective™ Process, for understanding the "true customer experience." It's a process that includes a review of all of a company's communications, interviews with employees, and customers and prospects, and an analysis to gain a comprehensive perspective of the customer experience.

After attempting to personify your company, and after sifting through that list of attributes, characteristics, benefits, and beliefs that characterize your organization, you need to land on that "one thing" that distinguishes you from your competitors. What is your non-negotiable characteristic, the thing that gets employees up in the morning, that is unique to your organization?

Once you've identified your nugget, you can then work on articulating a statement that is a distillation of the key attribute of your organization, artfully worded to resonate with your employees. Your distinctive value, the nugget, puts your company in a position to develop a brand promise that "sings."

Drafting Your Brand Promise

There are some guidelines regarding how to frame your brand promise. It should be short, and it should be simple. Short and sweet is imperative, since anything that's longer than ten or twelve words is difficult for employees to remember. And if it's difficult to immediately recall and recite, then it's almost impossible to internalize, and that's part of the goal when drafting the brand promise.

Ideally, your brand promise should also be compelling, or at least an interesting turn of phrase. At Vox, for years we've based our brand on being "the voice of the customer." Notice we don't say "being empathetic to the customer, client, and employee." That doesn't sing! No, you need to create a phrase or sentence that catches the ear, and even more important, catches the imagination of your employees.

From "voice of the customer," we can elaborate as much as we want, but the anchor is that phrase. And new employees who are exposed to it during their first few months of training are then able to quickly—even subconsciously—make the connection to the inherent meanings of our mission, our vision, and our brand every time they see that phrase: "voice of the customer."

If you don't think you have a real brand promise, now's the time. So get going!

So . . . What Do I Do Now?

In this chapter, we examined the sometimes irrational nature of branding and the power of using metaphors to help develop a unique and powerful brand promise for your company. Here's how you can use the principles mentioned to hone in on an ideal brand promise for your company:

1. *Personify Your Company.* This doesn't need to be an extensive research project. Start with yourself. Paint a picture of who your company is. What are the traits that de-

fine it: humanistic, charitable, innovative, committed, cutting edge, traditional? The key here is to define it as it is, not as you'd like it to be. By fleshing out the personality of the business—as seen by employees, customers, and the general public—you can then decide if you can work with some of these existing attributes in order to build a brand promise and identity that are sincere and authentic. Only then can you create something that's consistent and built for the long term.

2. *Find "the Nugget."* It's there somewhere. We maintain that there is a distinctive and valuable trait within your organization, one that you can use as the linchpin for your core brand promise. Finding this nugget might not be easy, but it's well worth the effort.

3. *Build Consensus.* Does everybody on the senior management level really believe in the brand promise? If not, you're doomed. It's only when you have total buy-in, when everybody is on board, that you can successfully leverage the brand promise to drive consistent activity across all channels and functions within your organization.

Chapter 4

Customer Research: Just What Are Your Customers Thinking?

Your most unhappy customers are your greatest source of learning.

Bill Gates

When our company, Vox, was just starting out and had a limited number of customers, I wanted to know what those customers were thinking. So I did what owners of many other small companies do. I picked up the phone, called one of my few clients, and asked, "Hey, John, how are we doing?" If John said he was having some small issue with our service, I was able to immediately investigate and resolve the problem. And even if John said, "Everything is going okay," yet I sensed a hesitation in his voice, I could probe for particular issues with the relationship, our process, or our deliverables, to try to find out what he really thought. If, when I hung up, I still wasn't satisfied that John was thrilled with Vox, despite what he said, I'd call in the project manager on John's account and probe further. We could usually figure out if there really was an issue (for instance, if the project manager said he hadn't actually talked to John in the last week, that could be a problem). The lesson was: Just because John *said* things were okay didn't necessarily mean that John *thought* things were really okay.

Calling customers and asking for feedback may have been an effective method for understanding how they felt about Vox in its early stages, but of course as we grew, our customer base grew, as did the number of employees involved with any given account or customer. As a result, things got more complicated. And whether you're part of a small but growing company or a large corporation, understanding your customers is difficult. Add to that the other wrinkle that you might already know intuitively: For a variety of reasons, your customers sometimes avoid really telling you how they're feeling, even when you ask. The bottom line for any company is that, ultimately, it can't just email an individual customer, ask whether he or she is happy with your service, and treat the feedback received as reliable or actionable. There has to be some methodology, some process behind it. But creating a standardized quantitative (meaning empirical or numbers-based) method for capturing how customers *really* feel is easier said than done.

For many companies, large or small, that process for understanding customers is typically some type of customer satisfaction survey. Surely you've received these in all their various forms. Maybe it's a card in the hotel room asking you to rate your overall satisfaction regarding the cleanliness of the room, the friendliness of the staff, or the tastiness of the room service food. Or it could happen in the evening when you pick up the ringing telephone (without checking the caller ID first) and grimace when the person on the line asks you if you have "just a few minutes to answer some questions. . . ." Or, these days, it's often an inundation of email surveys, from the airlines to the credit card companies and others, offering up a series of questions that are to be answered by "selecting a number between one and five, with one being completely dissatisfied, and five being completely satisfied."

But while satisfaction surveys are ubiquitous, it doesn't mean they are the right thing to do. There are several reasons for this, which I'll delve into further in this chapter but mention briefly here. First, dissatisfied customers typically don't speak up, even when given the chance. Second, given the right situation, people lie. And the third reason relates to our irrational subconscious: Based on the way our brains operate, we can't tell the truth regarding how we feel even if we want to. With customer experience, and how it directly impacts on profitability, becoming a more and more important issue for businesses every day, it's imperative that companies not just go through the motions regarding customer feedback, but seek more innovative and effective methods for exploring how customers feel—at both the logical or conscious level, as well as the emotional, irrational level—in order to create actionable steps to drive a desired customer behavior (like purchasing) and improve the relationship.

Trending Toward Uncertainty

To be clear, I'm not saying that quantitative satisfaction surveys have no value at all. By creating a satisfaction rating baseline and then measuring your customers' satisfaction level on a regular basis (monthly or quarterly), you are able to identify trends. This information allows you to determine if satisfaction among your customers is increasing or decreasing, which is certainly good to know. There is a problem, however: You don't know *why* satisfaction is going up or down. And if you don't know why things are getting better or worse, there is no avenue by which you can specifically remedy or improve the situation.

Here's another way to look at it. Let's say you have an aquarium in your living room for your large collection of tropical fish. You have a full-time housekeeper (I know, neither do I) who is in charge of caring for the fish. You don't have time for feeding and such and don't really know the details because you are focused on other things like tennis and parties (apparently you're rich, congratulations). In fact, the only thing you do is wander by once a week and see if any of the fish are floating on top of the water. For several weeks, all the fish are swimming around, oblivious to your presence, but then you notice one angel fish floating on its side. You remove it to a proper burial/disposal and sigh. Then, over a series of weeks, it's two dead Tetra, then three Barbs.

Your "survey" tells you there's a problem. Some fish are clearly not reacting positively to their environment. You need to do something quickly. But what? Is it the type of food, too much or too little nourishment, the alkaline level of the water? Things are "trending downward quickly," but you have no idea what steps you need to take to correct course. And that's exactly the problem for a company when it notices that its satisfaction ratings—on whatever random scale it happens to be using—start to trend upward or downward. The customer experience, in some sense, is improving or deteriorating, but why?

Three Reasons It's Dangerous to Rely on Surveys to Measure Satisfaction

I've done several talks recently at industry events, discussing why traditional customer satisfaction surveys are notoriously unreliable as tools for improving customer retention. Some of those events have been a bit nerve wracking, as they included a number or market research professionals in the audience. Those professionals are part of an entire industry devoted to helping companies determine customer satisfaction levels through surveys and analysis. But just how much does your knowledge of "satisfaction" really add to your ability to keep your most profitable customers?

The answer is often, unfortunately, not much. While, as I mentioned, surveys do serve a purpose (primarily showing trending: "Are we doing better or worse than last year?"), I'll give you three fundamental reasons it's dangerous to rely on satisfaction surveys from irrational customers to help you improve the customer experience at your company.

Dissatisfied Customers Don't Speak Up

Yes, you get some of your customers to respond to satisfaction surveys. But which customers? And using which channels—online, phone, mail, email? Which customers bother to tell you about gaps in your service or lack of quality in your products? Is it your best customers, who make you the lion's share of your profit, or your worst customers, who you'd be happy to see leave? The truth is that many of your customers will never give you any insight into how they feel about your company, service, or products.

If you think about it, this makes sense. When you've been unhappy with a company that provides you with a good or service, do you try to somehow remedy the situation, to "fix" the company, or is it easier to just say "the heck with it" and take your business elsewhere? Of course, that doesn't mean customers don't tell anybody about a bad experience. Research shows that you'll share your bad-experience story with around fifteen people (mainly other prospective customers rather than the company itself). Interestingly, when customers have a feel-good story, they share it with only about half as many people.

I experienced this phenomenon first-hand with the business bank from which I recently "attrited." I do not like this bank. Of course, I didn't start out that way; it was a feeling that built up in my bile duct over the course of months, even years. When I first moved our business accounts to this particular institution, it seemed a step up from the community bank that—ironically—forgot I existed. This new bank was a major regional player, with many locations (one main branch was just steps away from my office), and it had offered me a large unsecured credit line—something the community bank was unwilling to do.

As a new customer, I'd stride over to the imposing, columned edifice, a healthy deposit in hand. Did I notice then, one might wonder, how slow the line moved? The loud ticking of the ornate clock high on the gilded wall as time slowly passed? Did it register that there always seemed to be just one teller working (usually dealing with a customer heaving up bags of change onto the marble counter) while several other employees chatted among themselves in plain view? Maybe, maybe not. But the branch manager, Kathleen, had personally solicited me, and I was always treated to a wave and a smile from her office, if not a "Hello, Bill. How's everything going?"

But, suddenly, Kathleen disappeared. She was there, and then she wasn't. I tried to call her and found myself in some imposter's voicemail. It was then that all the small irritants in service shifted from molehills to mountains. Finally, when someone pilfered a check intended for one of our contractors, and the bank didn't believe it constituted fraud, it was time to go.

I raise this episode to debate the concept of satisfaction surveys as a way of effectively monitoring the probability of retaining your customers. You see, during those critical months of customer disservice, as my brow furrowed and my hands clenched while waiting for someone in the lush bank lobby to condescend to sit down in conversation with me, I received several satisfaction surveys by email.

One might guess that I saw the survey as a way to puff out my chest and harrumph my way through the little check boxes and radio buttons that would virtually shout my dissatisfaction with said bank. Series after series of "2" out of "5" would be a clarion call for the bank to change its ways. Right?

But I didn't bother.

I didn't bother because . . . I was mad. I was mad, and I wasn't going to do them any favors. And I certainly wasn't going to waste one more minute on that place than I had to. And so, I did not register on their satisfaction radar screen.

In fact, I'm not alone in deciding that, instead of taking some time and providing guidance to an institution regarding my overall satisfaction, or lack thereof, I just leave. Several studies over the last few years have shown that, of the customers who recently left a company, only 4 percent ever bothered mentioning to the company that they had some sort of issue.[1] They simply used their feet to head out the door and to a competitor.

One could argue whether this general aversion we all have to providing satisfaction feedback to companies is irrational. It certainly seems, at the least, illogical, since companies often present the surveys as a way to improve aspects of their products and services, which in theory helps customers. Irrational or not, it seems to be a common tendency for the majority of customers to avoid direct feedback. And what many companies often overlook is that customers don't feel like they "owe" you anything, and they act accordingly.

If a customer is disgruntled with your organization, what's the easiest way for her to address the situation—by providing you with valuable feedback through your carefully implemented formal quantitative research tools, or perhaps by proactively alerting you to the problem in a way that you can record and measure?

No. Instead, she just leaves.

Customers Won't Tell You the Truth

Often, when customers do take the time to respond to satisfaction surveys, they'll respond that they are "satisfied" or "mostly satisfied" regardless of how they really feel. A study of people who recently left their banks illustrates this: 80 percent said they had been "satisfied" with their former institution. Of course, some people leave a bank because they have to move, or for some other valid reason—but not 4 out of 5.[2]

Why? What logical reason is there for somebody to mark "satisfied" when he or she is far from it? Simply put: It's easier. Also, the notion of "satisfaction" is a very soft concept. What does satisfied mean? For most, it indicates that overall you, the company, are, more or less, meeting expectations. Human nature is to be nice. If things aren't great, that usually spells "satisfied." And "satisfied" has very little correlation with loyalty.

Here's an example of what I mean. My wife Marti's car, an SUV (but I swear it's a fuel-efficient model), died on her one afternoon, in the middle of traffic, with two of our kids in the car. Needless to say, it was inconvenient and could have been dangerous. We had the car towed to the dealer, where I met up with Marti and we arranged for a rental. About three days later the SUV was repaired and I left work, met Marti at the rental car agency, and drove to the dealer. The cause of the stalling was somewhat mysterious, but the service department guy—let's call him Steve—said they had figured it out. As I was literally stepping over the threshold on the way out to get back to work, Steve said, "Mr. Cusick, is there any reason that you would not rate our service a '5' out of '5' when you receive our satisfaction survey?"

Of course, my main motivation was to get back to work, so over my shoulder I muttered "no," as I jogged for my car. After all, it appeared they had fixed the SUV and I needed to get out of there.

Two days later, it happened again: The car stalled, in traffic, with two kids in the car. The SUV was towed to the dealer, I met up with Marti and I disclosed to Steve that I was less than thrilled. More hassle. Two days later, Steve called and we went to pick up the SUV. On the way out the door, Steve said to me, "Mr. Cusick, is there any reason that you would not rate our service a '5' out of '5' when you receive our satisfaction survey?" I was irate. And yet, I didn't hesitate. "No," I snarled, doing my best to slam the door behind me. Why, you might wonder, did I not stop and go through the incredibly obvious reasons I was not satisfied? I was late for a meeting, I knew they couldn't "make me satisfied" at that point and that their motivation was not my satisfaction anyway, but the rating on the survey. And, I didn't want to "help" them in any way. Shallow of me? Probably. Irrational? No doubt. As we'll see below, we act irrationally, and are to a large degrees slaves to our subconscious inclinations, whether we know it or not.

Regardless of what was happening in my head at the time—rational or irrational—do you think my *behavior* indicated a "5" out of "5"? And when we shopped for a new car, do you think we went back to that dealer? (Hint: Don't put money on it.)

Even if Customers Want to Tell You the Truth, They Can't, Because They're Irrational

Customers are sensitive, emotional, largely irrational beings. How do we know this? Because research indicates that we are all emotional, irrational beings. We've learned just how irrational: *95 percent of our brain activity takes place in the irrational or subconscious;* the meager 5 percent that is conscious is often devoted to explaining (or "rationalizing") to ourselves why we act or feel certain ways after the fact. And we do this not by tapping into our subconscious, but by making inferences based on our behavior. In essence, we guess, and we make things up. This concept, that we can't access the actual reasons that we do the things we do, and so we infer reasons based on our actions, was originally put forth in 1972 by Daryl Bim, now a professor of psychology at Cornell University. It was a concept he named the "Self Perception Theory." Since then, a wealth of neurological research has reinforced the theory.

Because we are often guessing, we are poor judges of how we feel. And because we're making these inferences (or guesses) after the fact, without any access to the irrational subconscious, we're not very good at explaining why we behaved in a certain way. Put bluntly, we're often wrong. Timothy Wilson is a professor of psychology at the University of Virginia and a leading authority on the workings of our unconscious. In his book, *Strangers to Ourselves,*[3] he took the idea further in describing this inability to tap into the true reasons for our actions as a "fundamental attribution error." Just to be clear, this isn't a conscious or "rational" choice. There are certainly cases where we knowingly spin our story to avoid discomfort ("I stayed at the bar until three in the morning because I was concerned about my co-worker, who was drinking too much."). But more often, we are trying to be honest, and simply can't access the irrational reasons for our actions. The other factor here is that, although we're making guesses as to our feelings, we usually convince ourselves of our sincerity; in other words, we can't be convinced that we're just guessing.

There is a well-known study involving, believe it or not, pantyhose that illustrates fundamental attribution error. The researchers, Timothy Wilson (mentioned above) and Richard Nisbett, set up a table outside the entrance to a Meijer's Thrifty Acres grocery store in Ann Arbor, Michigan to, ostensibly, ask customers to do a product comparison on several brands of pantyhose. Four pairs of pantyhose were displayed side-by-side, labeled A, B, C, and D. The customers were asked to take a look, feel the products, and make a determination as to which pair was of the highest quality. What the customers did not know was that the four pairs were identical—same brand, same model.

After a careful inspection, each customer made a selection. One might think that—given the identical quality of the products—the distribution among the choices would be relatively even: around 25 percent each selecting A, B, C and D. In fact, there was a clear bias moving from A on the left to D on the right. The actual distribution was pair A selected by 12 percent, pair B by 17 percent, pair C by 31 percent, and pair D by a whopping 40 percent.

While there are some priming issues (which we'll discuss in Chapter 5), like positioning and arrangement of product displays, suggested by these results, the really interesting findings lie in the subsequent discussions with subjects. When asked to explain the reason for a particular pantyhose choice, most participants described assorted qualities of the "different" products, such as the material, sheerness, and elasticity. Nobody mentioned the position of the choice on the table, which, in fact, was the only difference.

As this experiment persuasively demonstrates, customers don't necessarily understand why they pick one product over another; in fact, some seemingly trivial considerations factor into a customer decision. After all, the order in which a product is displayed seems pretty trivial. This, then, leads to the obvious question: If customers seem incapable of latching onto the real rationale for the selections, what good does it do to—in a uniform, surface-level fashion—ask them their opinions?

Predicting the Future, with Your Eyes Closed

If, as we've seen with the self-perception theory and self-fabrication error, we're bad at articulating how we feel or what we think about a product or service, we're even worse at projecting forward, predicting how we will react to a certain situation. This may seem odd, considering that each of us supposedly has exclusive knowledge and access to our innermost feelings and desires. In fact, other people are as good—and sometimes better than we are—at predicting our future reactions and behavior in a specific situation or confronted with a stimulus.

We also have a tendency to overestimate how future events or circumstances will affect our mood, as if the event (or product or service) occurs in a vacuum. The phenomenon is called *focalism*. The gist is this: When we try to predict how we'll feel in the future, we do not typically account for the context of the situation. In another study by Timothy Wilson,[4] he asked a group of college football fans how they would feel if their team lost. The researchers found that participants typically overestimated the length of time that the results would affect their moods. In other words, people don't take into account all the other events, activities, and influences that will be "in play" at any given moment in the future.

These odd tendencies of ours would seem to cause some consternation for companies attempting to tap into the innermost motivations and desires of their customers. If most customers act on choices they make in their irrational subconscious, and yet can't tell us the real reasons for those choices (even if they are trying to be truthful), and, further, are unable to predict how they might behave in the future, we know at the very least that the traditional methods of customer research are wanting.

Behavior Is Truth

So, if typical quantitative opinion surveys aren't the answer to finding out what your customers are thinking, what is? Let's look at some innovative approaches to determining exactly what your customer base desires from you so that you can improve the customer experience and, as a result, drive the behaviors you're hoping for from your customers.

Look at the Numbers; They Don't Lie

The best way to understand your customers—in lieu of satisfaction or opinion surveys—is through direct observation of their *behaviors*. In a number of industries—banking, telecom, insurance—an analysis of retention numbers (how many customers are leaving and when) can pinpoint certain situations and contexts that are creating higher attrition (people leaving) without it being necessary to ask customers what they think. For instance, in financial services, retention is consistently lowest among first-year customers; it's also the time when customers are most likely to open an additional account or take out a loan. For a manufacturer, depending on the product being produced, doing some homework on *which* customers are buying *which* product *when*, and *how often* each customer buys, goes a long way toward establishing a starting point in terms of your understanding of what your customers really think.

I know this may seem almost elementary, but that doesn't mean companies are doing it. I remember a conversation I had with a bank company president who repeatedly told me that his customers "loved" the bank. His evidence was mainly anecdotal ("one of our best customers, Bob Smith, comes in and says hello even when he doesn't have any business") as well as based on the latest "satisfaction" survey. When I pressed on actual retention numbers, it was met with a dismissive wave and the utterance, "Our customers never leave. They love us!" Yet when we scratched the surface, we saw that many of the bank's customers were not necessarily leaving in a technical sense, but were leaving in spirit. For instance, instead of walking out the door completely, they were moving most of their primary accounts to other banks, but hanging onto a certificate of deposit because of the rate. That's known as partial attrition, and you don't see it unless you look closely at your numbers.

Watch and Listen

By doing some detective work in the form of direct observation of your customers' behaviors, a company can glean more about what is or is not effective within the overall customer experience, and then act accordingly. While it's perhaps not as clinical as some other methods of information gathering, it helps you bore down to customer experience gaps and opportunities.

For example, some hotels offer an increasing number of ways to check out at the end of a stay. You can go through the automatic check-out feature on the television in your room. Or you can walk down to the lobby and use the "Quick Check-Out" kiosk. You could also walk over to the front desk and do it the old-fashioned way, or do what I do, and just leave your keys in the room. Let's say that direct observation shows that, in a given day, 70 percent of guests are still walking up to the front desk and dealing with a clerk when they check out. What does this tell us?

We may not be certain, but it's telling us something, and we can take several more steps to find out more. It could be that the two other automatic methods for checking out (television and kiosk) are more cumbersome than we realized and cause frustration. Or it might be that we have exceptional people at the front desk who provide a warm, positive experience that customers see as worth the extra few minutes. So, it might be a simple technology problem that needs to be addressed, or it could be that we have a best-practice hiring process for finding great employees that should be introduced to other hotels in the chain. By noting our customers' behaviors in their interactions with the company, it's easy to see clues that we can turn into actionable steps for improving the customer experience.

Observation in the retail environment can be accomplished by, literally, watching your customers navigate the store. Does he or she blow right by the display in the entrance? Do customers seem in a hurry to make a specific purchase or do they linger in the aisles? Paco Underhill, a well-known speaker and author, describes himself as a "retail anthropologist." What, you might wonder, is a retail anthropologist? Basically, he explores the assorted influences and dynamics at play in the specific environments—particularly the retail situations—in which shoppers make purchase decisions. In his best-known book, *Why We Buy, The Science of Shopping*,[5] Underhill describes a bookstore where customers stopped at a bargain table just inside the door. They would scan the offerings, and many would make purchases from this display. A good sign, right? Not necessarily. Further observation showed that many of those customers were then not bothering to move further into the store to browse the wider selection of books available at list price or a smaller discount. Based on Underhill's recommendation, the "Bargain Books" table was removed and sales increased.

Think about if, instead of observation, the store had handed out a survey asking people if they "liked" the "Bargain Books" table in the front entryway. The feedback, one would guess, would be primarily positive, since it's obvious that the customers were taking advantage of it. But that didn't get at what the bookstore really wanted to find out: that is, is the "Bargain Books" section driving a particular desired behavior? That behavior might be, for example, higher sales per customer visit. Whether the customers say they like the table is almost irrelevant, in a way, to what the bookstore is trying to accomplish.

To Really Understand, Walk in Your Customer's Shoes

In our customer experience consulting firm, we provide another method to get into the customer's irrational brain without relying on satisfaction surveys. It focuses more on "walking in the customer's shoes." We call it a "Customerspective™ Audit." In short, we seek to dig directly into the real customer experience by reviewing all aspects of a customer's relationship with a company. We look at all advertising, promotional materials, customer communications, bills and statements, and the physical environment, walk through the purchase process, the "new customer" experience, and all manners of service through different channels (in person, online, and through call centers). We actually promise our clients that, just by looking at communications and processes, we will identify not just possible issues, but actual mistakes and problems that are keeping customers from expanding their relationship with the company. In fact, we found that the people least likely to truly understand what the customer is really going through are senior management within the company. Some of this isn't rocket science. If you take the time, for example, to just read the letters you're currently sending to your customers, you'll probably notice something that is at best irrelevant or boring, and at worst missing or incorrect information. The same holds for all aspects of the customer experience: Just look—it's surprising what you'll find.

In addition, we gain more specific insights by conducting qualitative, in-person interviews with current and, if possible, past customers, as well as front-line employees. The idea is to probe into specific impressions and feelings in a more open-ended way, following up on comments a customer makes with more questions. We don't ask questions like, "How satisfied are you?" Instead we focus on the customer's report of how he interacts with the company (past and present tense). It's easy for somebody to tell us that she walks by a store every day and wanders in only once every few months. Customers can tell us if they bought any products. There's no emotional subconscious-to-conscious interpretation going on. In a way, it's a "just the facts, ma'am," type of approach. We get at what customers are doing, and when, but also what they are not doing, and why. And while we note what people tell us, we can also, by sitting across the table, observe their behavior: how excited, or mad, or happy they are.

This approach can create resistance in the organization. We did a Customerspective Audit for another bank several years ago (one that crowed about its satisfaction ratings). In one of the executive interviews prior to our audit, a vice president mentioned that their customers don't really care about doing business online. "They like to come into the bank," he stated confidently. That assumption was a red flag to us. After completing the audit, in our presentation of the findings, we noted that, in five out of eight in-depth in-branch customer interviews, the customers described difficulty in the sign-up process for the customer section of the website, as well as frustrating limitations in the online banking, with several saying it was serious enough that they would need to change banks soon if it wasn't improved. The response from the bank president was, "Is that a statistically significant sample?"

Don't Ask "How Do You Feel?" Ask "What Did You Do?"

We still help our clients with quantitative surveys, but we never recommend that they focus on satisfaction. Instead, we design questions that are more focused on behavior. As we've seen, if you ask about feelings (i.e., "Are you satisfied with the service you received?"), customers are incapable of providing an accurate response. However, if you ask questions related to customer's and the company's behavior, the respondent is in a position to provide an answer that is closer to the truth. Keep in mind, however, that those answers are still based on the customer's perception, which can be a window into the subconscious. For example, if you ask a customer, "On average, how long do you wait in line for service at our store?" and then give several ranges, the customer will give you his or her perception of that time. If that perceived wait time is longer than we'd like it to be, we can work on specific processes around that issue to reduce wait time. Then, by repeating the survey regularly, we can see if our *perceived* performance is improving.

Another question might be, "How often do you visit our website on average each month?" A high number might be a positive or negative indication. Combine that with a follow-up question of "How many times in the last month have you purchased a product through our website?" (depending, of course, on your business landscape and goals). Those two answers can combine to provide you with a more accurate picture of where you need to focus attention than asking, "Are you completely, mostly, somewhat, or not satisfied with your experience on our website?"

When we design quantitative research, our starting point is to first understand the business goals, and then identify the customer behaviors that would drive—or inhibit—results. Customer research takes time and money, so don't spin your wheels!

"Standardized" Doesn't Necessarily Mean Effective

Of course, quantitative surveys have a place in your overall customer and market research efforts. But by looking at your customers' actual behavior (or, at the least, asking about it), you gain more specific clues as to where there might be issues. And by taking a further step back and reviewing what your actual customer experience looks like to your customers, you gain a better sense of where there might be more obvious problems or opportunities upon which you could take some specific actions. With the knowledge of overall customer behavior as well as your typical customer experience at hand, you can research on a deeper level, using both qualitative customer interviews and then quantitative surveys that ask behavioral-based questions.

There is a certain comfort for many companies in satisfaction surveys. They are relatively easy to conduct, you can just "job it out" to a vendor, and nobody needs to "get his hands dirty," digging in the dark corners or blind alleys within the web processes or obsolete language on customer service letters. Quantitative surveys don't force employees to look the customer in the eyes, to ask probing and creative questions, or to observe their behavior as they deal with the company. The problem is, you get what you pay for. "Satisfied" customers are great; customers who behave in ways that positively drive your company results are better.

And, in fact, by focusing on the specific behaviors of your customers, and then "walking in your customers' shoes" to truly understand the customer experience, you are doing the things you need to do in order to attract, embrace, and retain your customers.

So . . . What Do I Do Now?

So, now you know that your customers often avoid giving you feedback (even when they are unhappy), sometimes lie to you when they do respond, and aren't necessarily even capable of providing you with the truth about how they really feel deep down in their irrational subconscious. But there are effective methods for discovering how to best shape your customer experience in ways that will create happy customers who drive company profitability.

1. *Know Your Numbers.* What are your customer numbers? They're anything you can get your hands on: sales by store or by household; retention and attrition by customer segment; Web analytics. Numbers describe customer behavior, and behavior is the ultimate truth serum. The numbers are in your organization somewhere, maybe in other departments or areas. Be relentless and hunt down the numbers that describe your customers' behavior.

2. *Walk in the Customer's Shoes.* When we do it, we call it the Customerspective Audit,™ but you can call it whatever you want. The important thing is that you make a sincere effort to really understand what your customer experience looks and feels like. That means reviewing all your communications (from the glamorous print ads down to the monthly account statements); talk to your frontline employees (they know more than anyone about what might be driving good and bad customer behavior); observe customer processes (transactions; website interactions; customer service calls, etc.) in action.

3. *Embed Behavioral Questions in Your Surveys.* These questions are the next best thing to observing a customer's behavior. If you are conducting quantitative surveys, don't lean on the traditional "satisfaction" idea. Instead, design a survey that focuses on behavior. For example, ask through which channel a customer purchased from you last or how often the customer purchases your products versus competitor products. Give easy-to-answer ranges that can be quantitatively analyzed and can quickly point to specific products, processes, or communications that you can focus on and improve.

Chapter 5

Prime Time: How Framing and Context Shape a Customer's Experience

The customer perceives service in his or her own terms.

Arch McGill

We all like to feel we're in control of our emotions, our decisions, and our actions. Most of us are also convinced that we have free will, and that we consciously make rational decisions. It's human nature. Think of the decisions you make throughout the day. Surely they are based on taking in information and making reasoned, logical choices, aren't they?

But that's often not the case; it's just not how our brains work. The primary processing "machinery" that dictates our feelings and our behaviors is located in the irrational subconscious portion of our brains. We can't consciously access what is happening in the subconscious and, for a long time, we had no idea whether, or how, outside factors might influence our feelings or our decisions. However, research conducted in the late 1990s and early 2000s has produced the most convincing evidence yet that a variety of outside factors—some very subtle—

can strongly sway a person's behavior, often without any conscious awareness by the individual.

Understanding how these influences, known as *priming,* can impact—for better or worse—the ways existing or prospective customers might make decisions or behave is critical for succeeding in your marketing and customer experience efforts. Priming describes a phenomenon wherein a person is subconsciously reacting to an environment or stimulus that is inherently positive or negative. Let's look at some examples of this dynamic at work. Once we understand how it operates, we can explore what you can do to shape a customer's environment in a way that will encourage customer behavior that is a positive result for both your customer and your company.

Priming: A Simple Nudge Will Do

New Yorkers are known for their independence, their progressiveness, and their . . . assertiveness. But they aren't necessarily known for their patience. That makes the results of a well-known behavioral study conducted at New York University in 1996—cited in Malcolm Gladwell's popular book, *Blink*[1]— demonstrating the influence of priming all the more powerful. In this social experiment, conducted by John Bargh, Mark Chen, and Lara Burrows of New York University, the subjects were asked to come into an office and complete a word test. They were then randomly divided into two groups and given one of two tests. In one, the words were uniformly positive and sunny; in the other, they were generally of a negative nature. What the subjects didn't realize was that the experiment really started when they turned their test in and walked out the door.

After finishing the test, the subjects were asked to walk down the hall to ask the person in charge about the next assignment. This person, however, was engaged in a conversation with a co-conspirator. The actual test began with the timing of how long the subject would wait before interrupting the conversation. The results are startling (keep in mind this is in New York). The subjects primed with the negative test words waited for an *average* of 5 minutes before interrupting. Those who took the "more positive" test *all* were patient enough to wait a full 10 minutes, at which point the experiment was ended. Keep in mind that the only difference between the two groups was which test was taken. Clearly, the impact of priming is fundamental to the nature of our behavior. Of course, we're often not aware of that influence when it's happening. This raises interesting implications as to how companies would want to color the customer experience in order to encourage customers to stay or to buy. Do you understand how your customers are really reacting to all the different environments, communications, and interactions they must confront to do business with you? If companies really understood the impact priming might have on their customers, I would suggest that it also would encourage some much-needed introspection regarding their overall customer experience.

The Intended and Unintended Influences of Priming

You are being influenced through priming all the time. As you move through the world, external factors are constantly influencing your emotions, choices, and behaviors. Sometimes it is with intent, such as through the thousands of advertisements you are exposed to each day. Other times the influence may be totally unintentional, such as the effect of the color of a room, or the temperature of a person's hand you are shaking, and might have either a positive or negative impact. Let's take a closer look at how this might play out in a specific environment.

Imagine that you decide to take your spouse out for a nice dinner to celebrate your anniversary. You are warmly greeted by a smiling hostess, who wishes you a happy anniversary, and then walks you toward your white linen-covered table in a quiet corner. You've heard great things about the food here and that the chef is a rising star on the culinary scene.

As you are shown through the dining area, you pass the kitchen entrance and are slightly taken aback by a pungent odor. You catch it only briefly and then it's gone, although it hangs in your nose for a few more moments. Your spouse is happily telling you something and didn't seem to even notice. The smiling hostess pulls the chair out for you and you take your seat. The moment next to the kitchen is already forgotten. The rest of the evening goes smashingly—your waiter is attentive but not overbearing, the menu is filled with exciting choices, and the food is excellent. Or at least you keep telling yourself it's excellent. There's something about it, but you can't put your finger on it. Your spouse is beaming by the end of the meal.

In the next few months, when the subject of great restaurants comes up, you describe your experience there as "okay." You beg off going back with friends. You no longer have any memory of a smell that impacted your experience, but the impact remains. Such is the power of priming.

In our irrational subconscious, patterns develop. Specific groups of neurons fire when we are confronted with certain situations that we have encountered before. This subconscious firing produces moods, decisions, and behaviors. Thus, when you are confronted with a pungent smell, as in the restaurant, certain neuron patterns may fire below your conscious activity that prime you for bad-tasting food. Whether the food is delicious or not, your subconscious made the determination before the actual experience. This one small factor shaped the experience in a way in which you weren't aware. Think of different restaurants located near your home. If you live in an urban area, there's no doubt a number of them. Do you find yourself going to the same place over and over? What's the reason? Are there others that seem to be fine, but you have never bothered to give them a chance? There's a good probability that there is something about those eateries that is influencing your behavior, something that may be triggering a reaction in your subconscious, but that is nonetheless very real.

The Business Implications of Priming

The influence of priming—even in very subtle, nuanced ways—has been demonstrated clinically as well. There's an example described in a *New York Times* article[2] that illustrates how simple alterations in a person's environment can make a dramatic impact on his or her behavior. The experiment took place at Yale and was surprisingly simple but effective.

As subjects (college students) made their way into the experiment, each was asked by a conspirator in the hallway, bogged down with books, to help by holding his or her coffee for a moment. In some cases the coffee was hot; in others it was iced.

The students then were asked to read about and then rate a hypothetical person in terms of personality and characteristics. Interestingly, the subjects who held the iced cup of coffee prior to the experiment rated the person as being "much colder, less social, and more selfish" than the students who had held the cups of hot coffee. The scientists opined that this is a clear demonstration of how everything we see, feel, hear, taste, and smell can dramatically impact our emotions and behavior. Are the findings here, that a hot or cold beverage can directly impact a person's behavior in a measurable way, "rational"? On its surface, hardly. It's difficult to believe that we, without knowing it, can be so easily swayed. And yet the evidence on all fronts supports the theory. Given that, it's shocking how little thought or effort most companies have put into addressing the issue of priming and its potential influence over customer behavior.

Consider how your business interacts with its customers. If something as subtle as having a person hold a hot or cold beverage can potentially alter his or her behavior, imagine how a negatively tinged greeting might sour the results of a relationship. In our work with clients, we've encountered attempts to start customer interactions the right way—for instance, scripting the greeting of bank tellers so that each customer feels welcomed. It might be something like, "Welcome to First Trust Bank. How can I be of service today?" Or with the airlines rote: "We know you have a choice in airlines, and we appreciate your choosing ABC Air for your travel needs." In a way, these scripts are simply an attempt to prime the customer to feel positive as he or she begins the transaction. Theoretically, that makes sense. But if you've ever been on the receiving end of a clearly scripted greeting, you already know why it sometimes backfires. If the teller delivers a bored, disengaged greeting, no matter the words used, it fails to create positive feelings on the part of the customer. Worse yet can be the over-the-top "Up With People" cheerleader version of the greeting, which can come off as disingenuous.

You can't just go through the motions of priming your customers. There's no quick and easy solution. If the customer naturally is picking up on all the cues—both obvious and subtle—and those cues are cumulatively influencing how a customer feels and acts, then you, as the company must also make an effort to understand what those cues are and how the negative can be eliminated and the positive framed.

The Environmental Effects of Priming
on Customers

It's not just the direct interactions with customers that can potentially prime their irrational subconscious and influence specific behaviors. It's also the environment. Our surroundings are always changing and—subconsciously at least—we are always processing the different elements of that environment, which impact our emotions, our decisions, and our actions.

Take, for example, the retail environment. Consider the effects that priming within a store might have on customer behavior (buy or don't buy). The color of the walls, the temperature, the way sound travels, the music being piped through the store—there's no question it all serves to prime customers, for better or worse. The only question is whether management understands the influence of priming and is doing something intentionally to encourage a certain behavior (as opposed to unintentionally discouraging the desired behavior).

In his insightful book *Why We Shop,* Paco Underhill, the retail anthropologist we mentioned in the last chapter, highlights the importance of creating the right situations and environment for customers. Through field observation in a wide range of industries and locales, he notes all manner of gaffes in layouts, displays, processes, and behaviors that unwittingly prime the customer to avoid buying anything. For instance, Underhill describes a "butt-brush" zone in a store—a merchandise display in a tight traffic area where passers-by must physically brush by other shoppers. His observations showed that this "butt brush" understandably discouraged shoppers (especially women) from spending any time viewing the merchandise or, obviously, making purchases. It's important to note, I think, that the design of the store layout may have primed customers to avoid purchasing from that particular section of the store, but the only way to really determine that this was happening was to observe the actual behaviors in real time. Since research shows that people are rarely consciously aware of the reasons they act—or don't act—in a certain way, there's really no use asking.

Environment can create an irrational subconscious effect on people's behavior even when it comes down to important personal choices, such as voting. One interesting example involved the 2000 and 2004 elections in California. Stanford Graduate School of Business Researchers, doctoral graduates Jonah Berger and Marc Meredith and S. Christian Wheeler, associate professor of marketing, examined how the location of a polling place might influence a voter's decision making regarding referendums on the ballot in the two elections. Surprisingly, they found a measurable impact: Voters were more likely to vote for the school spending referendum if they were in a polling place located in a school. Even after removing certain factors (such as whether the voting district leaned toward the conservative or liberal), the polling place influence could be seen.

Whether describing a retail store or a polling place, these findings should get you thinking about the environment in which your customers interact and transact business with your company. That environment might be a physical place, like a store, restaurant, bank branch, or agent's office, or it might be a virtual space, like your website. (We'll get into a deeper discussion about websites in Chapter 7.) Can you confidently answer questions about your customer spaces? What do they look like, smell like, and feel like?

Priming and Framing

Priming may be viewed as a concept that describes how outside forces influence our emotions, decisions, and actions, sometimes in seemingly random ways. But assuming the effects of priming are random would be ignoring the evolutionary subtlety of our brain's inner workings. As we've discussed in Chapter 2 and elsewhere, it's impossible for our conscious brains to take in and process all the stimuli the world is throwing at us each second. We take in over eleven million bits of information every second; the rub is that the conscious portion of our brains can only handle about forty, so clearly, there's a lot going on under the surface. In order to survive and thrive, our brains naturally make connections and create patterns as a kind of shorthand way of processing environments and situations. Far from a weakness to be exploited, priming allows us to better negotiate our environment and interact with others, subconsciously reading cues and reacting accordingly.

Framing is a way of accounting for and utilizing priming. As explained by Gerd Gigerenzer in his book *Gut Feelings: The Intelligence of the Unconscious*,[3] framing "is defined as the expression of logically equivalent information (whether numerical or verbal) in different ways." In other words, it's a technique for presenting information in a way that will influence choice and behavior.

Consider a pricing quandary. Which offer is more attractive to you: "This week only—Save 15%!" or "This week only—Save $45!"? Unless you have very special sensory powers, you have no way of knowing which offer is more compelling. It all depends on the overall price. If the original price was $300, the company selling the product has a choice. Does it present (or frame) the offer as 15% or $45? It's the same thing, but the way we frame offers and other communications is a sort of priming that will influence your customers' choices and behaviors. Which is better? Without understanding your business, it's difficult to say.

Most likely you use the technique of framing every day in your business. Think about the last time you tried to convince a fellow employee to tackle some tough assignment. You probably had a choice as to how you would frame the task. It could be painted as a "problem" that needed to be addressed, a "challenge" for the employee to take on, or an "opportunity" for the employee to achieve. For most people, those three concepts prime a different response, with opportunity being the most positive and energizing.

A classic example of framing would be to consider how one might present a glass of water: half empty or half full? The words we use to frame our description can prime a person to feel either negative or positive about the product, the service, or the situation. This is a critical consideration in how you communicate with both prospective and current customers. Too often, in our experience, we see companies consider how they will frame their messages through advertising and marketing in the customer acquisition efforts, only to abandon framing as a consideration once a prospect becomes a customer. Companies that spend millions of dollars on their advertising put almost no thought into framing their more mundane communications, like billing statements, email confirmations, renewal letters, or user guides, missing a tremendous opportunity to solidify or grow customer relationships. Is your company guilty of this neglect?

The Impact of Context in Customer Decision Making and How to Use It in Your Business

Whether talking about priming or framing, the common denominator seems to be *context*. That is, the surrounding information and stimuli—whether we know it or not—directly impact our behaviors and the decisions we make. So the question to you is, do you want to let things just happen, or would it be better to try to actively control the way your customers encounter and interact with your company?

In the last chapter I mentioned a well-known behavioral experiment involving pantyhose. A majority of the subjects, when asked for their preference of four identical pairs of pantyhose, selected choice D. There is no other explanation for this than the context of the situation. When presented with an array of choices, people tended to lean on an existing, subconscious (and irrational) pattern to choose option D. While product companies have always known that shelf position within the grocery store, for instance, can impact sales, there's been less work done to determine positioning as it relates to the idea of priming. Think about when you run into the grocery store on the way home from work in order to buy, say, a jar of salsa. If you're like me, you don't buy salsa every week and aren't particularly brand loyal. You know you want "medium" heat, but after that you're lost. Does the positioning of the different brands within the array on the salsa shelf have some influence over your selection? Absolutely! Do I know which salsa you might purchase? Absolutely not! But if you are a company that makes and markets your own brand of salsa, you need to take the impact of priming and context into consideration as you negotiate with grocery chains for shelf space. As Timothy Wilson's pantyhose experiment shows, there's more to it than simple logic.

So how do you figure out your contextual puzzle? An initial step would be to review the research that already exists on this subject. The work of Paco Underhill can help you uncover significant lessons on how to set up an effective retail space. Just the appropriate use of color can significantly impact customer behavior. The right (or wrong) color on product labels, for instance, can have a tremendous priming impact in a retail context. Red, for example, seems to elicit warmth and tension (good for a print ad for a sports car!), while green symbolizes tranquility (great for a brochure for a spa).

Consumer product companies like Procter and Gamble have been researching the science of labeling for decades. If your product is geared at customers watching their weight, for example, certain lighter, more pastel colors tend to work. On the other hand, if you are producing a premium ice cream (with very different connotations than low-calorie foods) those colors might not work at all. The key is to scour the existing research that's already available and then test your messages, colors, etc. in order to observe what effect your priming efforts are producing on customer behavior.

It *All* Matters

If there's one lesson we can learn by looking at some of the research and findings in this chapter, it's that "it all matters." Because we are subconsciously absorbing and processing everything around us in a particular experience—the temperature, the colors, the tone of voice, the smell, etc.—and all those stimuli are priming us for behaving in a certain way, companies must confront the fact that "it all matters." The layout of your retail store, the wording in your customer letters, the tone of voice of your call center representative. All of it.

Obviously, it's impossible to account for every little nuance that a customer might encounter, every small factor that could prime a customer to stay or leave. But in my observations in talking to and working with different companies, many don't even attempt to understand how the "softer" aspects of customer experiences impact on their behavior. Surely, based on the experiments cited above, one can extrapolate that warm words (or warm coffee, for that matter) might influence a cus-

tomer to stay a little longer or to leave feeling a little more positively about an interaction. Can you shape your communications and experience in a way to perfectly prime your customers
to behave in a desirable way? Probably not. But that doesn't
mean you should ignore the possibilities, as many companies
do. Instead, take advantage of what we do know about our customers and about how different aspects of your communications, environments, and interactions might begin to influence
certain feeling or emotions.

So . . . What Do I Do Now?

If, in fact, we are all influenced by the myriad stimuli we encounter as we confront and interact with the world (and, by extension, with your company), it's safe to say that everything you
do as a company will have some impact on how your customers
feel and act. One of the things I do not recommend doing is simply asking your customers what they feel you are doing that is
positive or negative to the overall customer experience. While
you should feel free to speak with them, it cannot be the only
way you gather information. It's better to focus on the following steps:

1. *Acknowledge Priming's Potential Influence.* It's important
   that you stress to others in your company that the concept
   of priming is a very real thing. It exists, and as a busi-
   nessperson you need to recognize that the sometimes subtle ways (intentionally or otherwise) in which you interact
   or communicate with customers will influence their behavior positively or negatively. Only after convincing others in your company that this is important to bottom-line
   results will you be able to address the issue.

2. *Walk in the Customer's Shoes.* I know, I've mentioned this before. But it's critical that you understand what your customers are actually experiencing when they deal with your company. Now that you know how "every little thing" might have an influence on a customer's behavior, it makes sense to conduct your own Customerspective Audit, and pay special attention to how you may be priming your customers to behave in a certain way.

3. *Test, Test, Test.* The only way to be certain you understand the impact of your priming and framing efforts is to try different things and then verify the impact with your customers. Folks in direct mail understand this approach, as they typically will test one approach against another. Think about ways you might test one approach for priming in terms of communications, website, or retail space against another. Remember the proof is in the customer behavior.

4. *Establish Standards.* As you look more closely at your customer's typical experience as he or she interacts with your business, you'll begin to figure out ways to encourage desired behavior and avoid aspects that discourage the wrong behavior. As you make these determinations, the key is to meld them into the institutional knowledge of the company. Create a list of standards, which can be everything from the color on the walls in your retail space to the font you use on letters to your customers, in order to ensure some consistency in the customer experience. Yes, you probably already have standards, but were they created with a sense of their effectiveness, or were they developed arbitrarily, for reasons like "that looks nice"?

Chapter 6

Irrational Ain't Stupid: The Emotional Component of High-End Purchases

Follow your heart, but be quiet for a while first. Ask questions, then feel the answer. Learn to trust your heart.

Anonymous

We think we're so smart. Whenever we have a big decision to make about an important purchase or life choice, we take care and analyze the various features and benefits. If we're really smart, we might put together a pros and cons list, weighing each positive and negative. Then, after careful analysis, we make the appropriate decision or selection. Right?

Wrong. Think about some of the most important decisions you've made in your life: what college you'll attend, your career path, your spouse. Ultimately, was it all about the pros and cons, or did other factors enter into your decision? If you really think about it, didn't it come down to something that's hard to put your finger on? For the really important stuff, some might say that they weren't analytical or rational in the slightest, but that they "followed their heart."

As we'll see, there is strong evidence that we do, in fact, follow our heart when faced with decisions that really make a difference in our business and personal lives. And this has some strong implications for how your company should talk about its products and services to its customers.

The Power of the Hunch

The fact is, we *are* pretty darn smart in terms of how we make decisions about things like houses, investments, colleges, or cars—that is (ironically), as long as we don't consciously think about them too much. Indeed, there's evidence that we actually make better decisions, even on more complex, important problems or choices, by gathering information and then just letting it all stew. What's more, forcing ourselves to articulate our "rational" thought process for a decision will often lead us astray. The problem is that we cannot articulate all the positives and negatives involved in making a choice: Some are simply inaccessible, buried in our irrational subconscious. When we try to diligently plow through all the factors included in a decision, the result is that we get distracted from the real issues, which often leads to making a poor choice.

Professor Antonio Damasio, in his book *Descartes' Error*, suggests that all choices are really emotional, powered by the subconscious, and that we ultimately make all decisions using only one criterion: *"How will I feel if I do that?"* We have all hesitated at one point or another when trying to decide between two alternatives. Let's take a simple example: the choice between a minivan or a sports car. If you have a growing family, one option might seem like the "smart"choice, the choice that "anyone in his right mind" would make when reviewed analytically. But ultimately the criterion, as suggested by Damasio, is: "How would I feel if I bought the minivan?" or conversely, "How would I feel if I bought the sports car?"

If you are, above all else, an incredibly selfish or uncaring person, you might be able to pick the sports car and say to yourself, "I feel great!" But most of us would go with the more sensible choice, knowing that, while not being the most exciting way to go, it would result in a feeling of satisfaction, of doing the right thing. No matter the choice, the determining factor is not just the logical, conscious evaluation; it's the subconscious processing of what emotions the selection will evoke.

Customers Do Their Due Diligence, Then Go with Their Gut

Many companies are in the business of persuading people to make major purchases, anything from refrigerators to home theaters to RVs to diamond rings. It's not just in consumer goods, either. Some companies must convince other businesses to purchase big-ticket items in the form of capital expenditures—like printing presses or computer networks—or services, such as legal casework or advertising campaigns. At Vox, similar to other professional services firms, our challenge is to persuade companies to pay us for consulting engagements, which can add up to a substantial amount of money and time.

In any of these cases where somebody must "pull the trigger" and make a large purchasing decision, there is a need to provide solid, rational information regarding the features and benefits of your product or service. Nobody makes a decision that involves a significant investment without doing what many call "due diligence" (in other words, a thorough investigation). Still, research into our irrational subconscious shows that we don't really make these decisions through a dry, conscious analysis of the different features and benefits. We may take in all of that information, but it's in the irrational subconscious where the real "thinking" is going on. It's below the veil of our awareness that our hunches, gut feelings, or emotions ultimately point us in a particular direction.

How Intuition Can Trump Logic

This subconscious processing of decisions doesn't just occur in situations where people take their time and methodically evaluate alternatives. "Going with a hunch" is an effective decision-making strategy even in instantaneous situations.

In *Sources of Power*,[1] Gary Klein cites an example of how the human brain can take in and process a number of factors in a few split seconds during a complex situation, and the person can make the right decision. This instance involved a fire commander answering a call with his crew for a kitchen fire. Upon entering the house, several factors just didn't add up. For instance, it was hotter than it should have been, but there was very little smoke or flame. Also, the kitchen fire didn't react the way it should when water was applied. He was suddenly convinced something was not right and he yelled for his crew to get out. Moments later the floor collapsed. It turned out that the fire had not originated in the kitchen after all, but had started, and had continued to burn, in the basement. The firefighters had not even been aware at the time that the house had a basement. While the commander had made the right call, when asked to explain his quick thinking, he—seriously—attributed his hunch to "ESP."

What's going on here? How could he make the right call, almost instantaneously, without even understanding how he was doing it? It's the incredible processing power of our irrational subconscious.

Thinking It to Death

If we're pressed to analytically decide on a choice, and then to articulate our reasoning for the selection, we can influence ourselves into making an unsatisfactory choice. Professor of Psychology Timothy Wilson[2] describes an experiment in which two groups selected pieces of art to take home for several weeks. Members of one group carefully analyzed their choices and listed specific reasons for selecting a particular painting. Members of the other group simply selected paintings that they liked without articulating the rationale. Several weeks later the two groups were surveyed to see how satisfied they were with their selections. Surprisingly (to some at least), the group that was not required to provide reasons for their selections were happier than those who had to explain their choices when they made them. The finding suggests that we know what we want until somebody asks us to articulate our reason, then our decision-making ability begins to deteriorate.

The study shows that, at least for subjective decisions, we're better off making a selection simply because we "like it." If this is the case, then it would seem to be at odds with how we're taught in school to evaluate our choices. Now think about how your company makes decisions on important investments or purchase. There is usually some research involved, perhaps even a request for proposal (RFP), if it's a particular service you're looking for. You need to get all the relevant information that you can. If you are in charge of a small company, you might mull over the choices, you might even sleep on it, and ultimately "go with your gut." After all, you don't have to rationalize your choice to anybody else: You're in charge. But in a larger company, there are usually more people and processes involved. In fact, for most corporations, there is somebody from the procurement department who must make a recommendation on a vendor or product, with an accompanying rationale, justifying the choice. As the previous example suggests, this might be a poor way to make those decisions. Allowing some "hunch" factor into the process could help larger companies avoid rational but poor decisions.

The challenge for all of us in selling our goods or services is twofold: First, we must provide enough solid information and rationale to make our product or service a "safe" choice. As the old saying goes, "Nobody ever got fired for hiring IBM." Second, we must connect on an emotional level with the decision maker. Easier said than done. What about for you? What are you doing to make a real connection, to play to not just the logical rationale of your prospects, but to the emotional side as well? Your challenge is to be the choice logically, but also when the prospect "goes with a hunch."

At Vox, we feel this challenge acutely. We are a smaller consulting firm doing business with much larger companies. It's a constant challenge to balance the sheer heft of many proposals—in terms of the "justification" for engaging our company over others—with the ability to "keep it simple" and make a real connection. While we've often been successful, our approach is constantly evolving.

"He Seems Like a Perfect Fit . . . but No Thanks"

Several years ago we at Vox stumbled on this principle of "intelligent, irrational decision making" without realizing it. At the time, we were growing quickly, but we were also struggling with finding the right people to fill new positions. It was really the first time that other employees, besides my key vice president (who happens to also be my sister) and I, were involved in the interviewing process. The result was that we would both meet more briefly than in the past with the job candidate after others had done preliminary interviews and made recommendations. In general, the candidates seemed to fit the positions in terms of qualifications, education, and experience. But there were times where one of us just "had a feeling" one way or another about a candidate. "I don't know," I might say. "I can't put my finger on it, but something seemed odd about that guy."

"Like what?" my sister would press. "He graduated cum laude. He knows the business. I liked him." And I would relent. It usually took several months (sometimes less) for the flaw to become obvious to me, to my sister, to our employees, and to our clients. The flaw was often something related to personality and attitude (i.e., something that doesn't pop up in a resume). This would happen the other way as well, with me pushing and Jeannie shrugging, with the same result.

So we came up with a solution. We granted ourselves peremptory veto power. If there was just "something" that was niggling at our brain about a candidate—game over. It sounds harsh, but we've found it's less so than telling an employee he or she is being terminated after two or three months. This is, of course, on its face hardly a rational approach. But given what we know about how we all think and analyze choices, irrational seems to be the most intelligent strategy.

Consider the same rationale if you have a spouse or significant other. What was your initial reaction when you first met him or her? Did you reserve your feelings one way or another until you could run through some sort of checklist of "qualifications"? Some people talk about "love at first sight." I think most of us would acknowledge that how we are attracted to and eventually even marry another person has little to do with ticking off requirements or creating a pros and cons list. In a way it's much more complex, and in a way it's about following what your gut tells you.

We would all agree, I think, that a choice like who one decides to marry is both incredibly important and deeply emotional. In a way, like many other important customer decisions, it's a purchase selection. We don't look at it analytically at all. In our irrational subconscious, there is an evaluation going on that drives those emotions. Your subconscious can quickly bring to bear all the lessons and experiences you have gleaned throughout your life and, without your conscious awareness, apply these lessons to the decision at hand. So, for important choices we make, the evidence strongly suggests that we use that same strategy for weighing our options: trusting our gut. It turns out that we're right to do so.

The lesson for you and your business is pretty clear: If you make important choices with your gut or, in other words, your irrational subconscious, so do your customers, or prospective customers. This isn't a trivial consideration when trying to design your marketing and sales activities to gain new business.

No Matter the Product, Sell the Emotion

For businesses large and small offering products or services, selling is a question of both the rational and irrational. And given our knowledge of how people really make these purchase decisions, it's easy to see how, no matter what the product or service, you are really selling emotions. If a decision is being made, emotion is driving it.

It's almost a cliché in sales these days that you first have to establish a relationship and build trust before you can get to a sale. In consulting this advice is ubiquitous, espoused in countless books by a wide array of experts. The reason this cliché persists is that it's true. One of the sharpest, most common-sense experts on the subject is consultant David Maister, who has written extensively on the management of professional service firms. In his book *The Trusted Advisor*,[3] he advises that step one in new business development is to "earn trust" rather than to wow the prospect with the bells and whistles of a product or service. The most important thing, Maister says, is to make a more personal connection.

Although Maister doesn't delve too deeply into psychological detail, his view is consistent with the irrational subconscious approach. No matter who the customer or decision maker is—the user, the procurement department employee, etc.—the ultimate decision is an emotional one. We don't buy things from people we don't trust or, just as important, don't like. This may seem less than logical, but there's a clear reason for it that's been wired into our brains over many generations of evolutionary development. At its most basic, it's a survival instinct: Only interact with people who appear to wish you well.

The message is, I think, clear on this count. If you sell through any type of personal approach, you must establish a relationship first and foremost. Earning trust is the only way to move to the next level and get the prospect to answer in the affirmative the question "If I choose them, how will it make me feel?"

Analysis Paralysis: Why More Information Doesn't Necessarily Help Your Customers Make a Decision

I can't think of a more arid, logical purchase decision than investment products (of course, it could just be me). If there is an arena in which customers can dive deep into an ocean of factors and drown in analysis, it's the investment industry. The complexity of choices, strategies, forecasting models, and general prognostication causes some to ignore it entirely, others to turn to professional advisors to make their investment decisions for them, and yet others to spend a great deal of time trying to dig in and understand the "science" of it for themselves.

One might think that, of almost any industry, a clear-headed, analytical approach—considering all the factors and data possible—would be best in making your stock and other investment selections. (Granted, nobody's been great at this in recent years.) Apparently, however, you would be wrong. In *Gut Feelings: The Intelligence of the Unconscious*,[4] Gerd Gigerenzer describes just how effective (or ineffective) one can be in picking stocks, and how it's not necessarily related to the amount of expertise or analysis applied.

In 2000, the investment magazine *Capital* conducted a stock-picking contest. It set out 50 stocks from which over 10,000 participants could buy, hold, and sell for the term of the contest. Many conducted extensive research and analysis to select an optimal portfolio. Gigerenzer and economist Andreas Ortmann tried something different. They conducted a random survey of people who were largely ignorant of the stock market, asking simply which stocks on the list they recognized. They then simply picked the ten most recognized stocks for their portfolio and, in essence, let it sit there through the duration of the contest. So, how do you think they did?

In a down market, the portfolio they selected still gained 2.5 percent. This compared to one of the preeminent experts in the field—the editor of *Capital* magazine—whose portfolio lost over 18 percent of its value in the same timeframe. On its face, it's really a shocking result, but it's not an anomaly. They repeated the test with similar results and came to the same conclusion: People who are not well versed in the stock market, who simply picked stocks based on what they had heard of, consistently beat experts, some of whom make a living advising others in their investment choices. What does this mean?

Even though this was a portfolio built on the collective contributions of a number of people, the principle is consistent with other findings and models how our irrational subconscious works, specifically: that consciously considering a large number of factors when making a potentially complex decision is a good way to get it wrong. Instead, by gleaning what you can about a problem or decision, and then going with your gut feeling, you are allowing your subconscious do the hard work of eliminating the superfluous information, the distractions that that don't really matter, so you can focus on what does.

Take a look at the websites of many of the larger companies in the investment industry. Whether they're companies that sell products (Schwab, Fidelity, Nuveen, etc.) or the advice around investments (Morningstar, Motley Fool), the general approach is to provide lots and lots of information. That in itself isn't a bad thing, it's just not really the right thing for its irrational customers.

As we've seen in several chapters, the important factor is to present the relevant information in a way where a customer can end up with a decision that he or she feels good about emotionally. To make that deeper connection, you must persuade the customer to answer the question, "How would I *feel* if I did that?" in a positive way. In order to do that, you need to provide the customer with enough information to allow her to make a confident decision, but also helping her eliminate many of the distractions that don't matter so she can "go with her hunch." Whether they know it or not, that's exactly what your customers are doing, so why not make it easy for them? You still must present all the information, but whether presenting it in a sales meeting, in the mail, or on the Web, it needs to be organized without distractions.

Buyers Lie

For many of us, the purchase of a home is one of the most significant decisions we're ever going to make. It's a major investment, and it will dictate to a large degree our quality of life (close to work? three bathrooms? two-car garage?) for years to come. But is it a rational decision? Most home shoppers create a list of the amenities, location, style, etc. that they require. Given the possible features available these days, those lists can get long.

Several years ago, when my wife Marti and I were shopping for our current home, there were some things we saw as requirements. We wanted to stay in the same town (Oak Park, Illinois, which borders Chicago) that we were living in at the time. It's a village with many old Victorians edging the tree-lined streets, but also with the elevated train running through its center—a direct connection into the city. We were looking for something bigger than we had, with more bathrooms, as we were up to three children. Ideally, we were seeking a house in nice condition, not requiring much work, located northwest of the village square, in what was considered the "better" section of the town.

Our real estate agent, Joe, nodded and smiled as we gave him all the parameters for our new home. He was a friend, someone who understood my wife's creativity and tastes. (Marti is an interior designer.) He didn't push back on any of our requisites. Several weeks into the process I got a call at work from Marti. "You have to check out this house." She sounded excited. "You have to go straight from work, and Joe will meet you."

I sighed. It was the middle of a cold and gray Midwest February, and I had been looking forward to just sneaking home and relaxing. "Where is it?"

"Only five blocks from our house (not exactly where we had agreed we were looking). It's on a cul-de-sac" (rare in this town), "and it's going on the market tomorrow." The market had been very hot at the time, so any decent homes were being sold, typically above asking price, within several days. "I really like it." I knew that meant I was probably supposed to like it, too.

I went to the address, and then did a double-take to make sure I was in the right place. You could barely see the house through all the overgrown weed trees in the front yard, but what you could see was downright scary. It was, by far, the worst house on the block; that was evident before I even got out of the car. The roof of the tall, narrow old farmhouse appeared to be sagging. The entire structure was covered in an ugly green asphalt siding. I looked up at the deteriorating chimney, near the peak of the roof, and could swear I saw a bird fly up and disappear inside the house.

Joe met me and said, "Give it a chance." I gave him a tight-lipped grin/grimace, and we went up to the covered porch and in the creaking oak front door. The inside was, if possible worse to my eyes than the exterior. The wooden floors were all severely worn, all the century-old oak and fir trim was beat up and almost black with age and abuse over the years. The small, dark kitchen had greasy pink Formica cabinets. Much of the plumbing and electric was either dangerously worn or inoperable. The loudly humming refrigerator looked to be flush against the back wall of the kitchen, but further investigation revealed it was hanging through a hole in the wall into the unheated mud porch, which itself was drooping off the back of the house. The stairs to the second floor leaned to the right, the bedrooms were small, and the cavernous attic was dark—save for the light shining in from the holes in the walls—and I heard some distinct rustling noises, which I took to be either squirrels or birds, but realized it didn't matter either way.

Needless to say, we bought the house immediately.

Surprised? I was, too. Irrational? No question. After all, if you had looked at our list of "requirements" at the start of the process, this house met few, if any, of them. But in hindsight, I really shouldn't have been surprised. While I saw the flaws in the house, my wife saw an incredible opportunity to create something special. It was on a wonderful, quiet street, on an extra large lot (both unusual for Oak Park), it was just a few blocks from a grade school, the junior high, and the high school (something that, strangely, wasn't part of our original list). But perhaps, most important, the house had "great bones," as my wife would say in referring to the layout and potential. When she saw the house, she saw a place that was something more than a rundown structure; she saw what it could become—our home. And, over the course of several years, that's exactly what it became. In fact, I'm in our spacious, sunshine-filled kitchen, in that once-horrible house, as I write this.

We apparently aren't alone in starting with one idea of what a new house should be and ending with a completely different one. Real estate agents ask people what they are looking for, and their clients come back with a list of features that they "can't live without." But, of course, they can live without many things. They just don't know it. They're deceiving themselves and their agents. Timothy Wilson relates a similar story in *Strangers to Ourselves*, saying that there's even a phrase agents use for the shoppers: "Buyers Lie."

How does your company deal with "lying" customers? Surely, this isn't only happening in the real estate industry. The first step, regardless of your product or service offering, is to acknowledge that you are working with irrational customers. What they are initially telling you they need may be a far cry from what they ultimately decide on. This happens constantly to us at Vox. Just because a customer knows she has a problem does not mean that she can articulate the true issue in the first few conversations. It's up to us to dig and creatively ask questions to get to the meat of the customer's issue or challenge or need. Is your company taking this into account as part of the selling consideration?

So . . . What Do I Do Now?

The lesson to be learned is that, no matter how large or important the decision, we all process our choices emotionally within our irrational subconscious. The implication for companies is that they must take a second look at their sales and customer processes, possibly stepping away from the feature-benefit nature of many promotional materials, for example. While cold, hard features are still necessary (after all, we still need to rationalize to ourselves why we made a purchase, after the fact), we recommend pushing on the emotional aspects of a product or service, even if in some industries that might seem counterintuitive. It's easy to see how emotion is front and center if you're trying to sell perfume, but what about insurance, or hardware, or investments? Absolutely!

1. *First, Build Trust.* It's not an easy, cookie-cutter solution, but in order to succeed in selling major products or services, you need to be aware of the importance of building trust. *The Trusted Advisor*, by David Maister, provides an insightful approach to earning a client's trust. You need to change the perspective of your sales team to focus first on building a relationship that provides value to the client, even (or rather, especially) before a sale is made.

2. *Eliminate Distractions.* Of course you must provide all the information your customers need to make intelligent decisions, but you must do it in a way in which you are

creating a hierarchy of that information so that it allows the customer to separate the wheat from the chaff. List a litany of product or service features if you must, but do it in a way (using organization into categories and intelligent design of promotional materials, for instance) that doesn't make the buyer's decision more complex. Simplify everything.

3. *Creatively Interrogate Your Customers.* Your customers lie to you, albeit unintentionally. They may be certain, in their logical consciousness, that they know exactly what they need. But you need to dig deeper to get at the real issue they are trying to resolve. It doesn't matter if you're selling cars, houses, or consulting engagements, don't start the sales process with a value proposition, start it with questions.

4. *Incorporate Emotion into Your Sales Pitch.* I know, this is easier said than done. But it's critical that, no matter what you're selling, or to whom you are selling, you design your sales process so that your customer can answer the irrational or emotional question, "How will I *feel* if I do this?"

Chapter 7

A Web of Issues: Online Users Know What They Like, but They Can't Tell You

The real problem is not whether machines think, but whether men do.

B.F. Skinner

One would think we were beyond the need to explain the importance of the web channel as a way to attract, sell, communicate, and provide service to your customers, but I know it depends on what industry you toil in and the current space your customers occupy, so let's review just how valuable your website could be to your overall business. Then we can look at how your customers, through their irrational subconscious, think about and interact with the Web and finally how you should go about developing your online channel so that it makes a true connection with them.

The Web Channel: "Virtually" Priceless

The mistake many companies still make is viewing their websites as some sort of "thing," like a great print ad or, if you're further along, a television commercial. The truth is that it doesn't really matter what industry you're in: Your website should be seen as a key element or conduit in your interaction and relationship with your customers. And it must be viewed—always—in the greater context of the overall customer experience.

A fantastic website only helps you if it works seamlessly with the other channels through which your customers interact with your company. These might include personal interaction, your call center, mobile (text and Internet) communications, email, snail mail, and your website. We would argue that the Web is an avenue of opportunity for you to interact with and serve your customers regardless of whether that's been the case in the past.

If it's designed and built with a constant focus on your customers, the site creates an incredible synergy: Customers can get things done more quickly, access their accounts, find important information immediately, and connect with other customers; the company, in turn, enjoys a stronger relationship with the customer through more frequent customer visits to the site, and potentially, immense efficiency and cost savings. Why wouldn't you want to invest in moving your website to the next level?

"I Owe It All to My Computer"

We have always had an interesting relationship with our technology. Remember being introduced to "HAL," the computer on a Jupiter-bound spaceship in the film *2001: A Space Odyssey?*

HAL interacted with the crew, including Dave, the ship's commander, as he moved about the ship, chatting back and forth about issues like ship functions and their overall mission, even playing chess at one point. (We'll ignore the plot device in which HAL ends up killing all but one of the crew members). At the time (the movie was made in 1968), this seemed like quite the stretch in the relationship between man and machine. But we have a tendency to imbue our technology with human traits, and that creates an emotional connection.

Researchers have gained some interesting insights into how we're drawn to technology and, more recently, how we interact with it. In one 1996 study, Byron Reeves and Clifford Nass[1] demonstrated a phenomenon they call "reciprocity." The experiment shows just what it suggests. Users were observed working with different computers, some with a PC that had "helped" them previously (i.e., performed some task) and others with a computer that hadn't "helped" them. It appeared that users were more willing to reciprocate, or provide more help, to a computer that had previously helped them than to a computer that hadn't. This sense that the study participants "owed" something more to one computer over another hints at a dynamic we can exploit to enrich the user's experience with a website.

It may be irrational, but our observations support this premise of reciprocity: We interact with and come back to websites that are *doing* something for us. This might include connecting us with other people who have a similar interest, or allowing us to easily shop for shoes, insurance, or industrial circuit boards, or to check our accounts, or to "click to chat" with a real person. In other words, we're willing to spend more time and effort on sites if the return is worth it.

What we've seen is that there is a tremendous opportunity for almost any company to develop web channels that enrich the customer relationship. It's almost ironic, but the truth is that technology can add humanity to your overall customer experience. In *How Customers Think*, Gerald Zaltman describes how people tend to attach or "tag" an emotion if it's memorable. So part of the goal for any website is to make the content, individual interaction, and overall experience connect on an emotional level, and therefore memorable.

That technological connection to companies and others is represented these days through the Web. It's beyond the scope of this book to address all the ways the Web is changing and expanding, but it's most likely clear to most readers that the Web is no longer limited to traditional websites. Tools like LinkedIn, Twitter, Facebook, and others can enhance the breadth of your online presence beyond your company website. In addition, mobile "apps" (applications that can be used anywhere through a cell phone, such as online banking or account management) are exploding in certain industries. While you're focusing on how to develop a website that resonates with your customers, you owe it to yourself to become educated in these forms of customer acquisition and service.

Feel the Love: Build Emotion and Connection Through Your Website

You may not be one of the rabid customers of Zappos.com, the Internet retailer, but you probably know someone who is. Zappos, an online shoe store started in 1999, is one of the relatively few unequivocal Internet success stories. While not yet as well known as Amazon and eBay, Zappos is a study in how to successfully create a Web experience that is more than just a website—that is, in fact, a complete experience. The company has grown in less than ten years to sales approaching one billion dollars, and there's no sign they'll be slowing down anytime soon.

When Zappos started, the idea of selling shoes on the Internet was not something many people would predict for success. Think about how you buy shoes. You might go to a nice department store like Nordstrom, or one of those shoe warehouses to find a deal, or to your favorite specialty shop to support the your local merchant. But with shoes there's one constant: You get to try the shoes on. Given that this is a fundamental part of everybody's shoe-buying experience, it's surprising that Zappos managed to launch in the first place.

How do you sell shoes when your customers can't try them on? If you are a website, first you make it incredibly easy for customers to get the shoes, and Zappos does that by providing free shipping. And while they offer delivery within four days, they do their best to deliver the customer's order within one to two days. This harkens back to Chapter 3, where we discussed the brand promise and setting expectations. By setting a particular expectation (free delivery in four days), Zappos can easily "hit the bar," and most of the time it can beat it, delighting its customers (and therefore, according to Zaltman, creating positive emotion and making the interaction memorable). In addition, Zappos has a liberal return policy. You can return a pair of shoes, with free shipping (you print out a label off the website) for literally any reason, no questions asked.

Zappos does more than simply make it easy to get its shoes, though. It also makes it easy to contact them with any questions or concerns you might have. If you have a question, you can call the Zappos contact center anytime 24/7. The customer service people are well trained (there's a full two-week program all trainees must survive before soloing with customers) and are highly engaged. I'll talk more about how Zappos hires and trains to create engaged employees in Chapter 10. Suffice it to say that when you call Zappos' customer service number, you are not routed on an endless loop by an IVR

(Interactive Voice Response) system like so many companies. And as you talk to one of the company's reps (again, these are employees, not "hired help" contracted through an outside agency as many companies now prefer as a more "efficient" practice), you get a real sense that the representative wants you to be happy at the end of the call. For one thing, you're not rushed through the call (a common call center practice). The reps are empowered to be flexible enough to deal with your particular situation. For another, if you say you don't like the sandals because the color is a little different than it seemed in the online pictures, you can just send them back, no charge. Is the size off? Just send them back. They'll ship you back another size immediately, free of charge. And if there is actually a quality issue, they may not even bother you with sending the faulty pair back; they'll just fire out a new pair right away. Zappos trusts you. Let me repeat that. Zappos trusts you. Imagine how that makes you feel as a customer. It's a powerful sentiment and emotion that connects with people at a very deep level.

Even in companies where the website is the central hub of the company, the engine for the prospecting, sales, and service of the enterprise, to be successful there must be a comprehensive approach to serving customers. No matter the channels of interaction, the goal is to create a positive feeling for when the customer asks him- or herself: How does associating with this company make me feel? And Zappos understands that—Web company or not—the true customer experience is the cumulative effect of *all* interactions and communications on the customer's perception of the company. Conversely, even if the website is not the primary component of your business approach, you should consider in what ways it can be integrated to add to the overall customer experience.

Doing, Not Just Reading

One of the things we notice as we work on the web channels of companies in more traditional industries is that a fundamental mistake is made regarding their websites at the very beginning of the discussion. It's a mistake that sets development of a site on the wrong course, essentially guaranteeing that the end result will never be an optimum solution. That mistake revolves around how they anticipate their customers will be utilizing the site.

Instead of trying to understand how the customer interacts with the company, and then integrating the site into the overall experience (including ways for the customer to actually accomplish tasks, communicate, learn, and more through the site), the company sees the site as a platform that floats out on the sea of the Internet on its own. If customers should find their way to the site, there are often some interesting graphics to look at, perhaps a couple of cool tools to keep their attention for a few minutes, and possibly even a video. The site is a marketing device, and nothing more. It's always discouraging when we're helping a company rebuild a website and the client's attitude is, "well, we can just use or 'repurpose' the existing content for the new site." That attitude defeats the purpose and wastes the effort involved in creating a new Web experience.

Emotion, as we've seen, is created in the irrational subconscious. We may be guessing at our reasons for why we act the way we do, as Timothy Wilson, Gerald Zaltman, and others have demonstrated. But it's also clear, through experiments like the hot coffee priming test in Chapter 5, that how a company interacts with customers creates strong emotions that directly impact customer behavior, for better or worse. Companies like Zappos understand that. Of course, the website must deliver a seamless experience. But it's more than that. The customer perception is the cumulative effect of all customer interactions and exposures with the company.

"Oh, Behave!"

In Chapter 4, when discussing customer research, I argued that asking customers what they think doesn't do you a lot of good. The reason? Given how our irrational subconscious works, we are largely incapable of accessing the "truth" and providing a straight answer. We are forever rationalizing, explaining to others (and even ourselves) why we behave the way we do. This being the case, we found that the best approach to gaining insights into what your customers want (or don't want) is by extrapolating from their past or present behavior. Behavior is the ultimate truth serum.

What does that mean on the Web? Luckily, there are a variety of ways to determine just what your customers (or your competitors' customers) are embracing or avoiding. Web analytics—the discipline through which you can observe and analyze user behavior—is an entire industry now, and you can delve into exactly how users maneuver through a given site. You can see where customers came from, where they landed on the site, how long they spent on the first page, where they went next, for how long, etc. The data available also allows you to study your competitors, and benchmark your performance on the Web against theirs.

There are successful companies that understand how to observe and analyze user needs based almost exclusively on their behaviors. Aside from Zappos, the obvious example is Amazon.com. I'm sure there are some of you who don't use Amazon; I'm guessing you are in the minority. Think about some of the aspects of your experience as you shop for books, blenders, or baskets: as soon as you've spent just a little time on the site, you'll start to notice clues of Amazon's voracious curiosity about your behavior. For instance, almost immediately after you land on a specific product page, you'll find a message telling you "Customers who bought this item also bought:"

and see photos of several related products to "help" you with your shopping experience. Amazon nudges you toward products you "might be interested in" throughout the page. It's important to note that it's not just your Web experience they are focused on; it's your entire shopping experience, because the folks at Amazon realize they aren't just competing against other websites for your attention, they're also trying to top any other alternative you have, including walking down the street or getting in your car and driving to the mall.

Another feature Amazon provides is aimed at a customer's cumulative behavior over the past several visits. When I land on the Amazon home page, the very top line of the screen reads: "Hello, William Cusick. We have some recommendations for you." Based on my previous purchases, Amazon automatically compiles a short list of items I might be interested in. Of course, that can sometimes not be as effective as they might wish. For instance, during the Christmas season I do much of my shopping online, in addition to my usual purchase of books for leisure and for research. The result can seem, at best, schizophrenic. Last year the suggestions ranged from a cookbook (I barely ever cook) to running shorts (which made sense) and women's sweaters (hopefully, I don't have to say that I rarely buy women's sweaters) to a book on behavioral psychology.

Apple uses much the same strategy on its iTunes site. By simply observing user behavior, the company can extrapolate the selections—songs, videos, podcasts—that the user would more likely be interested in. Apple, Amazon, eBay, Netflix, and other companies may possess more resources to devote to these solutions, but you can use the same principles (possibly on a smaller scale) to add power to your web experience. Behavior is truth. How your customers act—what they shop for, and what functions they most often utilize—are evidence about how they will act in the future. By understanding that, you can take incremental steps toward encouraging the types of customer behavior that both leave your customers feeling positive about the relationship with your company and achieve the company's specific business objectives.

Hammers, Saws, JavaScript, and Applets: Building Your Site

At this point you might be thinking: Well, it's great to be able to observe behavior that's actually happening right now within your website, but what if you are trying to build something fresh? What if you have the opportunity to create a new experience for your customers through your website? You can, of course, look at what customers have been doing, on your site and others, but that doesn't necessarily give you insight into a more optimum experience, does it? It's helpful, but not prescient.

So, the big question is: Just how do you develop a website that is more than just a website? How do you, instead, create an experience, and even more, an experience that leaves a customer with the feeling that yours is the type of company that he enjoys associating with? It's an admirable goal, but given that your customers are irrational, you must develop a process that helps you tap into that subconscious to determine what users really want to get out of the site. It's more than what the site should look like. Rather, the objective is to determine what should the site *do* for the customer. In other words, does a customer need to find information, or to easily shop and buy things, or to check her account?

We have been working with clients and helping them create new web channels for the last ten years, and in that time we've seen how other designers and developers typically approach creation of a new website. Frankly, we often sense that they are missing the mark. Part of the problem with the typical approach has to do with the design mentality to creating the site. It's an approach that leads to sites that might look nice, but that don't work for your company. They don't appropriately engage customers, which is the least your site should accomplish these days. Design, of course, is a critical component of the site development, but I'd like to offer up some steps to ensure that your site is all that it can be.

Determine the Brand and Company Goals

It sounds simple and even obvious, I know, but you'd be surprised how often brand and company goals never enter into the conversation. There are some cool things you can do with a website, especially as it relates to the customer experience, but without first understanding what you want to accomplish, you can't create an experience that drives desired customer behavior.

In addition, as we discussed in Chapter 3, understanding the brand promise is critical to creating powerful, consistent interactions and communications (and your website is both) with your prospects and customers. Think about Southwest Airlines. The company brand promise is "The Low-Fare Airline." There are other components to the brand and the experience, but that's the core promise. Southwest understands, after years of observing its customers' behavior, that there are key aspects of the brand that are drivers of the desired customer behavior, and so they stay true to the story.

Take a look at the website: www.southwest.com. It's very simple to do things like search for and book flights. It's bright and cheery in terms of design. The content is consistent with the brand promise, as it highlights low fares and no hidden fees. No fees for checking extra bags, etc. There's a section titled "Fly for Less." It's all—the design, the tools and functionality, and the content—built around the central idea of "The Low-Fare Airline." Now take a look at some of the other major airline sites. On American Airlines' site (aa.com), a customer can accomplish many of the same things as on Southwest's site, but there is, arguably, no overarching theme or message that shines through in the experience. United Airlines (united.com) is similar to American: functional, but lacking any real identity or emotion. And remember, it's emotion that creates a memorable experience. No emotion equals nothing memorable, which often equals no customer loyalty.

Your brand serves to set your customers' expectations; it is how you present your company's distinctive value proposition. If you are clear about your brand, it allows everyone involved to work from a baseline expectation. And the result is more consistent and more powerful.

Create the Architecture *Before* Designing a Site

It's confounding to me that, often, the first thing a client will see from a developer, designer, or agency charged with creating a new site is a home page design where the navigation—the primary menu that typically runs across the top or left of the page—has already been determined, seemingly by default. How can this still be happening? Before any design is discussed, the company and developer must determine exactly how your customers, prospects, and possibly even employees, will be using the site. Before thinking about *how it looks*, think about *what it will do*.

For instance, a company trying to reduce the number of salespeople in the field should obviously think long and hard about the *structure* of the website. Building in a seamless purchase process, where a prospect can "pull the trigger" effortlessly on sales, would seem to be one of the primary components of that company's site. We often work with insurance companies, and it's surprising how often we need to gently move the conversation back to these basic points around the initial website strategy (i.e., deciding what you want the site to help you and your customers do).

Let me define what I mean by "architecture." Architecture is the "bones" of the site. Think of it as the blueprint. It shows the general layout of the site—the location of the kitchen, the bathrooms, the bedrooms, etc.—with a sense of how the elements are oriented to each other. For example, if the main entry is into the foyer (home page), how many doors must you pass through if you want to get a drink out of the refrigerator? To pull this metaphor a little further along, ask yourself what most people entering the house want to accomplish. Is it getting a drink, sitting and reading a paper, or doing their laundry? And, accordingly, is the house set up in a way in which visitors can accomplish their tasks or activities in as simple and efficient a way as possible?

If you successfully create a blueprint, or information architecture, for your site, it will make the development and design process much more efficient and streamlined. With some customer input (but only in the way described below), you'll be on your way to creating a site that elicits the desired behavior from your customers, which means you hit your company goals.

Test, Test, Then Test

Your customers will have a hard time articulating exactly what they want from your website. The reason is, in part, because they're incapable of tapping into their irrational subconscious needs. But perhaps more important, your customers (all of us) are not very skilled at projecting what they would enjoy or appreciate in the future.

However, if you are taking the right path to developing your website and not cutting corners, you've already clarified the company goals and brand promise, and then thought carefully about the architecture of the site, so it's time to build. The point of this chapter is not to get too technical, so we won't delve into specific software, programming, and other issues, and instead stay at a slightly higher altitude. Whether you utilize wireframes, just launch into general design, or build a clickable prototype, the key to a high probability of success in developing your site is to test, then test, and then test.

Some Web agencies or developers will mention usability testing as more of an option, as something that's nice to do. We don't see usability testing as an option. We consider it an essential part of the website development process. Most view website development as being a continuous process, working on the design from the start until the site is up, possibly with a usability test as the site nears completion. If someone recommends this to you, say no! In addition, if you have a current site and someone recommends sending out a satisfaction survey regarding the site, say no!

Instead, here's what we recommend for website creation: *frequent, small-scale usability testing.* Let me elaborate. We map out the development process for a website and, as opposed to the more traditional approach, include at least three to four small-scale usability sessions with just a few people involved in each session. The first would be very early in the process, possibly using cards or paper, to get a sense of whether the architecture we've developed makes sense to the end user. The next session might occur when we have the graphical representation of the site, possibly in a PowerPoint format that is easy to change. Finally, we might employ what we call a "clickable prototype" that is very close to the final website in terms of structure, appearance, and functionality.

And since just asking customers what they think doesn't usually give us insights, we focus all of these sessions on behavior. Even if just flipping through and organizing cards with key terms to help categorize content, it's important to ask the customer to do something, not just give an opinion. Whether it's finding a specific bit of information about your product, registering for a newsletter, or making a purchase, allowing the customer to navigate through the model of the site (in whatever form you can manage) provides tremendous insight to the developers as to what works and what doesn't.

Throughout these sessions, we are not using a large number of participants. In fact, we typically ask only three or four people at a time to run through the tests. For what we (and you) are trying to accomplish, this should be sufficient. The other major deviation from more traditional methods is that we often schedule three-day sessions. The first day we conduct usability tests (of varying degrees, based on where we are in the development curve). The second day we quickly review our findings from Day One and make quick adjustments to the site structure or format so that on Day Three we can test the improvements.

In this way we can make quick alterations to the site throughout the development process based on customer behavior and not wait until it's too late. You can do the exact same thing as you develop your new site, or refresh your existing site. The important things to remember are (1) frequent, small-scale testing, (2) testing on behavior, not just "customer opinion," and (3) making quick adjustments to stay on the right track. We've found that, using this method, we can be sure that as we near the completion of a website engagement, the confidence for success is extremely high.

When You're Done, You're Not Done: Incremental Improvement Based on Behavior

The method I described above is ideal for identifying "red flags," or major concerns regarding navigation, design, or usability as the site is developed. It will assure you aren't confronted by any major surprises when you launch your company website. You'll be confident that through your frequent, small-scale usability testing you'll have established a winning site.

But it won't be perfect. It won't be perfect because it's impossible, with small- or large-scale testing beforehand, to hit a home run when your site is originally posted, not requiring any changes for the foreseeable future. You need to see how it performs, and then start making incremental improvements. But how?

Again, the answer is to focus on behavior through Web analytics and what are called *A/B tests*. A/B tests have been used for years in the direct marketing world. It's a pretty simple concept. You put your "winning" website up (the "A" site), and then test new ideas or modifications by posting an alternative ("B") site. When a visitor types in your URL, he or she is randomly assigned A or B. This allows you to review through Web tracking tools how customers behave on each site, where they go, when they leave, etc. The basic idea is to continually test your "winning" model—the version of your website that generates the most activity for you in terms of a defined goal, such as hits or purchases—against a new version. Whichever one comes out on top becomes your new version.

On the Web, it's relatively easy, working with your Web host, to create an A/B test. The power of this method is twofold: First, you can continue to refine your site after it's up, incrementally improving different aspects to increase desired customer behavior, and second, you are using existing *customer behavior* to test your site. In other words, you don't need to lean on the unreliable method of asking your irrational customers what they want.

So . . . What Do I Do Now?

Your website can be a powerful tool for attracting and retaining your irrational customers, if you approach the development and refinement of your site with the right goals and methods.

1. *Integrate the Website into the Entire Customer Experience.* Your customers' perceptions of your company are based on the cumulative effect of all communications and interactions they have with your business. Whether your website is the primary or an ancillary component of your company's public face, you need to approach its development or refinement with an eye toward how it fits into the total customer scheme.

2. *Use Web Tracking and Analytics Tools to Understand Behavior and Needs.* Customers are irrational, and they can't tell you exactly how they feel about their experiences on your website. But their behavior points at the truth of how your website is performing. A wide array of tools are available. There are even free tools that are quite good. As with most things Internet, Google offers a free and effective web tracking application.

3. *The Key Is Frequent, Small-Scale Testing.* When developing a new site, it's critical that you incorporate frequent, small-scale usability testing into your website development process. Use what you have (cards, PowerPoint slides,

clickable prototype, etc.) to find the "red flags" in the structure, content, design, and functionality of the site. Focus the testing on behavior; make the user do something, then monitor the actual experience. There are firms who can help you with this, but make sure they are focused on behavior, not just customer opinion.

4. *Continue to Improve Your Site Through Tracking and Testing Customer Behavior.* Just because your website is done doesn't mean it's really done. It's never really done. You must track how your site is performing through Web tracking and analytics tools. But you can also conduct A/B tests that will allow you to test the performance of your site against a second approach, where Web users would randomly land on one of the two (or more) sites.

Chapter **8**

Phoning It In: Transform Your Phone Interactions into Powerful Moments of Truth

When people talk, listen completely. Most people don't listen.

Ernest Hemingway

Before the Web, there was the phone. And chances are that no matter the size or type of company, you still deal with your customers—in some capacity—over the phone. It remains one of the key channels for customer communications, whether you have five customers or five million. And by understanding that your customers are irrational, you can design your phone interactions in a way that resonates with them in helpful and beneficial ways.

If memory serves, while things have never been perfect, it seems that in the past, more often than not you could call a company and be speaking to a person within the first minute or two. I know—that was a while ago. Nowadays, a call into a large corporation usually is presaged by a customer taking a few breaths to gird him- or herself for the upcoming experience. Tentatively, the customer dials the 1-800 number, bracing for the, at best, imperfect interaction with . . . with what? With an obtuse, confusing automated system, one that might offer the friendly yet mechanized voice stating that "our menu has changed, so please listen to all of the options," or possibly a voice recognition system that says things like "I didn't get that. Did you say 'account status?'" as you repeatedly scream "representative!" into the mouthpiece in a futile attempt to talk to a human. How does that make a customer feel? Ready to punch a wall? I know that's how I feel, and I don't think I'm alone here.

But it's not just the ridiculous (to everybody but the company itself) automated systems companies have put in place. There is also the problem of *any* employee dealing with customers over the phone. In fact, the way that you and your employees come across has a tremendous impact on how your customers perceive your company. By understanding a little more about how we all think (i.e., irrationally), we can prepare our people and systems in order to create phone interactions (and, as we'll see, other real-time conversations) that help not just to create a positive feeling but to drive desired customer behavior.

We've All Got Needs: Maslow and Call Centers

No doubt, at some point in your high school or college days, you've come across the hierarchy of needs conceptualized by Abraham Maslow, the U.S. psychologist and a founder of "humanistic psychology." Presented in his 1943 paper "A Theory of Human Motivation," the model consists of five levels, which represent the "hierarchy" of a human being's physiological and psychological needs.

The lowest level of the hierarchy, physiological, includes our most basic physical needs—food, water, sex—followed at the next level by our safety needs, such as shelter. As each of these basic needs is met, the next level of needs on the hierarchy comes into play. As long as a need on the "safety" level, say shelter, is met, it's no longer considered a high priority for an individual, and therefore no longer serves as a motivation. As you move up the hierarchy, you'll see the needs become more social and psychological with "Love/Belonging" and "Esteem" becoming priorities. What we inherently strive for are needs that revolve around both how we want to be perceived by others, and then, at the top of the hierarchy, how we can become something greater than our present selves through self-actualization. The needs at each of the higher levels will serve as motivation for a person, ultimately *driving behavior*. And as we've talked about in past chapters, our goal here, no matter the customer interaction, is to drive desired customer behavior.

This is an important model to consider when thinking about your customer interactions, particularly when analyzing how your company deals with its customers over the phone. Many businesses are ineffective in creating positive customer interactions not because they are making the attempt and failing, but more because they aren't making an attempt at all. Sure, perhaps the company prods its reps to say "thank you" and "you're welcome" during the course of a customer call, but there's no purposeful effort to make the call a real moment of truth from the customer's perspective.

So, how can a company use a model like Maslow's hierarchy to create a more effective customer-employee interaction? You can consult Figure 8.1 to understand just what emotions you can attempt to elicit in a customer in order to make

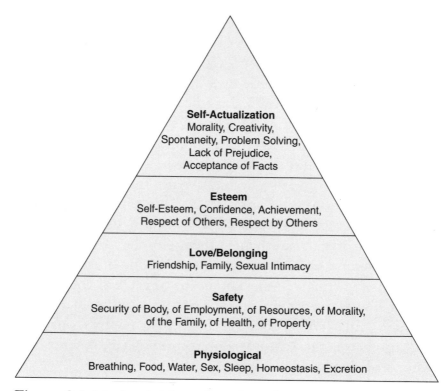

Figure 8.1 Maslow's hierarchy of needs.

the interaction memorable. The hierarchy shows that most companies could assume the basic physical and safety needs of the customer are met. But what of the next level—"Love/Belonging"? Belonging is a powerful motivation for almost all of us. It's a fundamental emotional force that produces positive feelings and memories. We all possess the strong need to feel welcomed into a group. It's a reason some are drawn, for example, to join sports teams, clubs, or church groups. Understanding just that one element can have a dramatic impact on how a company fashions its customer interactions.

Think about your company. What does it do to ensure that in its dealings with customers, it creates a strong feeling of belonging, a sense that you actually care about them? The absence of this connection can lead to anxiety (which is, in essence, the inability of the company to satisfy the appropriate needs shown in the hierarchy), which also drives customer behavior (away from your company). Imagine the impact on customer retention if, when a customer calls in, she is given a sense that you were in it with her, that the employee on the other end of the phone was really there to help her achieve whatever she was attempting to accomplish. How long does it take you as a customer, when you call in to a company, to accomplish what you set out to do, to determine if the phone call is going to leave you with a positive or negative feeling? It may only take a few seconds, but it leaves a lasting impact.

Create an Emotionally Memorable Interaction

If we hope to influence customer behavior, we need to tap into the emotional level within the subconscious. The interactions need to be memorable; otherwise, what's the point? In *How Customers Think*, Gerald Zaltman states that a memory is much stronger if it is tagged with an emotion. Your emotions are evoked in your subconscious. So it would seem that a goal for any moment of truth or customer interaction would be to evoke a strong positive emotion. And one way to set those goals would be to look to Maslow's hierarchy to determine whether you could connect emotionally with the customer on one of the levels shown.

An Ear and a Shoulder . . .

As an example, American Express does a good job of addressing several of Maslow's hierarchical needs in its phone interactions, particularly regarding the idea of belonging and esteem. Unlike some companies, when I call into its 800 number, there is a limited menu, and I don't get the sense that I'm running down a dark hallway where a wrong door chosen will result in a lengthy navigation back up to the entrance. Instead, I can be talking with a real, live person within a minute or less (which also says something about appropriate staffing). But the real value is in the exchange with the customer service representative. There's just 10 or 15 seconds of chitchat as the call is initiated, it's not scripted (which we all have the ability to see through very quickly), and it's just enough to allow me the confidence that I'm talking to an actual person.

However, the key to the call is that the customer service representative actually listens. Listening is a specific skill that gets short shrift in today's business world. You can tell the rep is listening, because throughout the call there are occasional utterances of empathy that go a long way toward a resolution ("I'm sorry you had that happen to you. Let's see if we can fix your problem right now."). The result is that the call is not just successful (i.e., I accomplished what I wanted) but pleasant and memorable as well. And those positive emotions typically lead to desired customer behaviors.

. . . Versus a Chore

Let's contrast that experience with one I had with Capital One. I was left a message to call back because of a "security issue," and I was given an 800 number. When I called, I found myself in the automated phone system. There were five options, with none of them being "speak to a representative." After pressing five for "more options," there were five more options, with none of them being "speak to a representative." Once again I selected more options, and the fifth choice was talking to a live person.

The amazing point here is that *Capital One called me.* I was minding my own business until *Capital One told me to call back.* Then it made me negotiate the back alleys of its phone system to speak with someone. And only when finally chatting with a human being was I informed that my "account information had been compromised." As it turned out, apparently somebody had managed to tap into the system and walk away with a bunch of account numbers, mine among them. So now, the representative needed to cancel my card. "Will you be sending me a new one?" I asked. "Yes, but you need to stay on the line while I take care of this," she replied.

"And when will I be getting that new card?"

"About seven days."

I snickered, since I can get a card in a day from American Express, but that's another story. The point here is that, in a way, Capital One succeeded, in that it created a memorable experience, albeit not one it would care to embrace. (It's interesting to note that I never received a new card from Capital One, forcing me to endure another phone call several weeks later, where Capital One claimed it had never talked to me, and therefore had not sent a new card. I was then put through the whole exercise one more time, just to add insult to injury.)

As we've seen, you can make a moment of truth memorable by tagging it with some sort of emotion. Ideally, you do that with an emotion that connects to a fundamental need, like belonging to a social group or increasing your self-esteem.

Conversely, you can also create a specific and memorable interaction by attaching to a negative emotion, which is exactly what Capital One had done. Yes, I will definitely remember the experience, and I will tell many others about it as well. But the experience was a negative one, and the emotion I felt was frustration, coupled with a bit of anger, and what I will be telling others about it in the future will not be bringing Capital One any new customers.

Expense or Asset? Designing an Irrationally Positive Call Center Experience

So, it's clear you don't have to be professionally involved in the industry to know that customer contact centers have a bad reputation when it comes to customer experience. You just have to be a customer. Who among us has not had at least one horrible experience dealing with a customer representative while trying to purchase or return an item, get a question answered, or schedule a service call? If we, as customers react irrationally and emotionally to these interactions, what is being done to address these basic human needs? While some companies have made progress, overall the system seems to be broken, and there aren't many obvious answers as to how to fix it. What is obvious is that companies of any significant size need a system, and there are tremendous advantages with regard to real-time data access and capture to allow a representative to view a full picture of the customer's account and history. But there are also tremendous challenges in systematizing everything involving the call center customer experience.

We cannot get too in-depth about the specific technical solutions or challenges with any deep level of nuance in this broad-based book, but there are principles that, if taken to heart, will keep you on the right track to both "take care of business" within your contact center and create powerful customer interactions. Remember, your goal is to not just efficiently process transactions; it's to reach down to the customer's irrational subconscious to generate positive emotions.

Don't Push Efficiency at the Expense of Emotion

As the technologies within call centers have advanced, so too have the techniques for evaluating their overall performance. Management and supervisors have grown increasingly analytical, scanning weekly and even daily reports on the center's productivity broken down by day parts, work units, and individual representatives.

The typical metrics that call centers employ include overall call volume, average call times, and average wait times. While these point toward efficiencies in operations, they tell us nothing about overall impact on customer retention. For instance: Is a 4-minute phone call with appropriate resolution a "better" experience for a customer than a 6-minute call with appropriate resolution? On its face, the answer seems to be clear. No customer wants to be on the phone with a company for more time than is necessary. The real answer is: It depends. In fact, research shows that fully two-thirds of customers will stay or leave a company based on their perception of the level of "employee indifference" in their first encounter (on the phone or otherwise).

If "indifference" is the real yardstick for determining whether customers are staying or leaving, if that's the real measure that will determine retention, and therefore revenue, why in the world do companies continue to look at their customer contact centers as expenses rather than profit centers? Many may pay lip service to "customer service," but then they measure employee performance on the number of calls handled in a given period of time, creating a tension for the employee between doing what's right for the customers by taking the time to be warm and considerate and doing what the company considers "high performing," handling as many calls as possible.

Efficiency . . .

The difference in approach becomes obvious when we look at two companies with distinct philosophies, Wal-Mart and Zappos. In September 2007, Wal-Mart decided that it simply didn't want its customers calling for certain situations, so it removed its 800 service number from its Web pages. This was part of what Wal-Mart, almost unbelievably, called its "Customer Contact Reduction" program.

This is an incredible move when you think about it. The 800 number listed on the website would have been used primarily by customers having some problem while dealing with the site. With no number, their only option would be to look to the site to help them out. Hopefully, you, as opposed to Wal-Mart, can see the problem with that. If you have a problem with online shipping of your product, for instance, and you are receiving an error message every time you attempt to determine the status, you have nobody to call who can help. It seems so obvious, but so do a lot of things when it comes to customer experience, and yet companies can't seem to get the concept that thinking about the experience from the customer's perspective makes good business sense. Can you guess whether Wal-Mart views its customer contact center as an expense or a profit center? My guess is that it saw the center as a "necessary evil," which led to the "logical" conclusion that the company could simply get rid of it.

... Versus Emotion

On the other hand, Zappos, the online shoe store discussed in the last chapter, takes a dramatically different approach. Its entire customer philosophy is built around the idea of delivering incredible service. It sees the customer experience as being *the whole thing*, not separated into different "experience vacuums," but rather fully integrated across its website and contact center. It's "customer service," not contact center service separated from Web experience.

It's essential that, if you have any type of contact center, you take a similar perspective. Your customers do not make a distinction. Imagine a customer of a fictional company, Acme Products. When a customer deals with Acme on the Web, he thinks of Acme Products as an overall company, not just its website. If another customer calls the customer service center, she thinks of Acme Products. You get the idea. This is an incredibly large issue for many companies these days. Many outsource the entire call center role, so that customers are calling into some vendor company with a small army of phone reps who handle calls for a number of different companies. You can imagine that trying to instill some sense of positive emotion into those experiences through training is close to impossible.

Zappos looks at the experience and sees its call center representatives as a fundamental component of the overall customer experience. We'll look at how it creates engaged customer representatives in the next chapter. But I hope you can see here that the overall philosophy is to get a customer to one of its engaged employees right away so they can begin to "Wow." There's nothing scripted about the interaction, just a caring employee who does whatever he or she can to make the customer happy, or even ecstatic.

"Is There Anybody *Out* There?" Why Automated Systems Are Not Helping

When you're talking to a customer representative or employee of a company, can you tell whether that person is really involved in the conversation or not? Most people would answer in the affirmative. I swear there have been times where I could *hear* the person on the other end of the phone yawn. There are countless ways to pick up on whether an employee, let's say a company contact center representative, is engaged, from the tone of the voice to the stilted or scripted nature of the responses. It's that tone (or lack thereof) that can determine if you decide to stay or leave as a customer. And remember, customers don't necessarily make that decision on a conscious level. The emotion created—positive or negative—has a strong influence on behavior, whether the customer realizes it or not.

Can an IVR (interactive voice response) system display "employee indifference"? Absolutely. It's clear to a customer when he or she confronts an automated system. There are many factors, both obvious and subtle, that create the customer experience and impact customer retention. But it's usually obvious. The technology can be fantastic, but there seems to be a dearth of thinking regarding the design of the experience. At some companies it appears as though there has been no thinking at all regarding the customer in the setup of the system. We preach to companies that they must "walk in the customer's shoes," but it's clear that has not happened yet when it comes to most companies' IVR systems. In fact, oftentimes the people who are least likely to have a real sense of the customers' experience are employees.

Just because a customer service representative is coldly efficient in dealing with customer requests, or worse—an interactive voice response system allows customers to solve their problem themselves—there's still a good chance that customers will sense employee indifference. Further, there are studies that show customers who have encountered a problem, and had an engaged employee quickly fix the problem, actually are more likely to stay than customers who have simply been correctly dealt with. Consider the alternative: The primary reason customers leave a company is the perception of employee indifference. This suggests a strong correlation between the caring, human interaction and retention.

Online Chat: The New "Call Center"

Many companies are attempting—through company structure and technology—to integrate their sales, service, and customer interactions across channels. For instance, we have worked with businesses that are installing a new "back end" system (to better manage all customer, transactional, pricing, and process information) that can be accessed by employees in a variety of customer-facing situations, and through the call center, email, or most recently a "click-to-chat" function on the Web. Click-to-chat is a feature that allows a customer to "talk" in real time with a company service representative through the website. I include mention of it in this chapter because the dynamic of "talking," even though it's by computer, is similar to how an exchange with the call center might be conducted. The same rules regarding emotion and creating a positive memory in the customer's subconscious must hold.

My wife Marti sent me a brilliant example of a click-to-chat conversation she had with a company I've already mentioned in this book: Comcast. Below is the actual transcript from that online real-time conversation, but let me set the stage. At the time we had been living at the residence in question (still our home) for about seven years. We had been cable television customers of Comcast for that entire time, and also users of Comcast's broadband cable Internet service. Marti wanted to *expand* our service by subscribing to a few premium channels like HBO, and possibly switch to the higher quality digital service. In other words, her intention was to *pay* the company *more* money each month. See if you can spot the point at which there is any empathy from the representative. In fact, see if you can spot the point at which the representative asks Marti exactly what she needs help with. The only things I've done are alter our contact information and the representative's name, and cleaned up some typos. Enjoy.

JANE: Hello Marti. Thank you for contacting Comcast Live Chat Support. My name is Jane. Please give me one moment to review your information.

JANE: Can you please confirm your address and phone number, so I can process your order correctly? Thanks a lot.

MARTI: 123 South Main Oak Park, IL 60302. 708-555-1234.

JANE: I am sorry however we are unable to process your order at this time. The previous resident(s) at the address you entered has not yet disconnected service. In order to resolve this issue, we need you to go to your local Comcast office so that proper verification of the change in residence can be recorded. You will need to bring a copy of your lease agreement or title of ownership to one of our in-person payment centers for verification.

Would you like the location of the closest Comcast store?

MARTI: I am the resident of the house. We have lived here for seven years.

JANE: You already have service. Is this correct?

MARTI: We want to change our Comcast cable service.

JANE: What is the name on the account?

MARTI: William J. Cusick.

JANE: No, I'm sorry this is incorrect.

MARTI: What do you mean it is incorrect?

MARTI: I pay the bill every month, I know we have a Comcast account.

JANE: Well, that name that you gave isn't right. Do you have the account number?

MARTI: You haven't sent the bill for this month, so I don't have the account number. Our address and phone have not changed.

JANE: You will need to go into the local office because the information that you gave me doesn't match. [Analyst has closed chat and left the room.]

It's not a call center, but the same principles apply. The dynamic is almost identical. What happened here? In the cable industry, after a few years, chances are a customer is extremely profitable. The cost of acquiring the customer is long since past. Further, the company doesn't need to spend a lot of time or money on customer retention efforts. Really, beyond providing the cable service itself, the bottom line is that the company just needs to be nice to the customer when it gets the chance, and the odds are the customer will stay around. But companies still don't get it. Do you?

Spinning a Yarn: Reinforce Your Customer's "Life Story"

Our irrational subconscious is always working, monitoring our reactions, influencing emotions, and dictating behaviors. It's that inaccessible area of our brain that dictates how we feel, how we act, and who we associate with. One might wonder how the subconscious makes those decisions. Some of the influence in the subconscious is based on our past experience and identifying patterns (which push us toward a "yes" or "no" decision). But what's really interesting is how we make sense out of those experiences.

As we make our way through the day-to-day of our lives, we are constantly confronted with situations and circumstances that we must deal with. These situations or challenges are often random events. Consider your past week. Surely there were certain instances that were planned, and in which you had some sense of how you were going to act, such as a business meeting. Then you might have faced other situations that came out of left field. Perhaps somebody on the crowded subway you were riding home started to harass another passenger. What do you do? Do you step in to break up the argument or do you turn away? Or perhaps you were expecting a promotion, and it went to another employee. How did you react? And why? If you're like most people, you'll look back on certain aspects of your week—and your month, your year, and more—and see it as a linear story, with over-riding arcs and themes.

It's your "life story."[1] It turns out your customers—as well as you, me, all of us—are constantly telling life stories. We are all subconsciously spinning out a narrative, trying our best to fit each interaction and experience into the bigger picture of our lives. It's this narrative that helps us clarify the self-image of who we are. We see how we've acted in past situations, the people we associated with, the causes we worked for to better define who we are. Again, you'll note, it's about past behavior—we look at what we did in the past, not just what we thought—that will help us dictate how we'll act in the future.

So, just what does understanding the fact that we all create life stories to define ourselves have to do with customer experience, particularly as it relates to call centers? Through our life stories, we create a self-image. That self-image is, in essence, is the answer to the question, "What type of person am I?" Customers will choose to do business with your company, or not, in large part by answering the question, "Is this the type of company that somebody like me would do business with?" Think back to the Apple/Microsoft comparison in Chapter 3. As we saw, there are definitely "Apple people" who identify strongly with the brand. A large part of that identity comes through in how customers perceive they are being valued and treated, and that can come across loud and clear in telephone interactions. What can you do? Think about your company brand promise and what you know about your customers. What is a typical customer life story? How do you fit into that story? If you can imbue your phone interactions with certain aspects of your brand that you know your customers identify with (independent thinker, green, conservative, exclusive, penny pinching?), you can create a strong emotional attachment between your company and customer that will influence the relationship.

The Most Important Employee:
The Receptionist?

As I mentioned earlier, communicating over the phone is not just the realm of the corporate call center. It's any time any of your employees talks to a customer. That happens in most companies, big or small, every day. Many companies don't have and won't need full customer call centers, but the principles in this chapter apply to anybody who answers a phone in your company. Do you spend any time at all talking to or training your employees on best exploiting this critical communications channel?

Kraig Kramers, a "serial CEO," who has engineered a number of impressive company turnarounds, as well as being an author and speaker, understands the importance of putting the right person with the right training at the very front of your company. He calls the receptionist your "most valuable employee." If you think about it for a minute, you can see the truth in that statement.

He or she is the gatekeeper of the company, and also the person who—more often than not—creates that all-important first impression. As Malcolm Gladwell demonstrates in his book, *Blink*, the first impression is incredibly powerful in creating a long-lasting perception for the caller and can also be very difficult to overcome if it's negative. Given that, think about the first impression your frontline person or people are giving to people calling in everyday. Is it positive or negative, or don't you know? If it's negative, you are doing your company irreparable damage, and you need to take steps right now to improve the situation. If you don't know, you need to find out.

Listen, Listen, Listen

In previous chapters, I've described "walking in the customer's shoes" as one of the most important steps you can take to improve customer experience. And it's not about to stop now.

For communicating over the phone, listening is the key. It works with call centers, where you can monitor live calls with customers. But it also works with any employees who deal with clients or customers.

With a call center, depending on the size and sophistication, you can listen to tapes, listen on-site in real time, or listen remotely to live calls. There are companies that allow executives in the company headquarters to listen in on live conversations right from their offices. And with other frontline employees who deal with customers or clients, you can easily monitor select calls through any basic phone system. This allows immediate coaching on not just the knowledge of the employee regarding the customer issue, but just as importantly the attitude and tone that's being projected.

Don't let yourself get mesmerized by the technology and systems that are promoted as a "magic bullet." Yes, these solutions can help to both increase efficiency and the information management of customer interactions. But they don't really do as much as you might think to create emotional, memorable interactions that will drive behavior.

So . . . What Do I Do Now?

Your real-time interactions with customers—whether through everyday phone calls, customer service call centers, or click-to-chat technology—present a challenge, but also a wonderful opportunity to create positive, memorable interactions. If approached with the right principles (not necessarily just as a question of cost and efficiency), you can shape the experiences to drive desired customer behavior.

1. *Focus on Emotion, Not Just Expense.* So many companies view a customer contact center only as an expense. If, as

Marshall Field once said, "Your customer is your only profit center," wouldn't it make more sense to view your customer contact resources in the same vein? By seeing the call center, and every call center interaction with a customer, as an investment rather than an expense, you can create completely different approaches to call handling. Is the representative who talks to the most customers in a day really your best employee? I doubt it. Rethink your call center metrics and individual performance incentives.

2. *Walk in the Customer's Shoes Through Your IVR or Menu System.* Yes, it's the same principle we talk about when considering all other aspects of customer experience, but that's because it's important. Call into your company call center and run through different customer scenarios with the IVR. Pay attention to the time it takes to accomplish something, but just as critically, consider how the interaction makes you feel. Are you happy or encouraged, or are you frustrated?

3. *Train Your Employees to Smile and Empower Them to Act.* When looking at your own call center operations, think about the Zappos approach: Of course you should employ the best technical solutions for being able to access and capture customer data; technology should be at the beck and call of the customer representative. But leave the strict scripting of calls to other companies. It doesn't work. Instead, focus on training your employees to understand what's really important about the call (the customer's contentment). And empower your representatives with the tools and incentives to make things happen for the customer.

4. *Enlist Management to Listen "in the Customer's Shoes."* Seems absurdly simple, doesn't it? As I've stressed throughout the book, the way to understand how customers will

react to your company is to walk in the customer's shoes. If your company maintains a call center of any kind, you need to do more than scan reports on productivity. And it needs to be not just you, but other members of management who commit to understanding the true customer experience. The senior executive team must make the effort to monitor real conversations between customers and call center reps (or frontline employees, or receptionists).

Chapter 9

Form or Function: The Power of Emotional Design

A common mistake that people make when trying to design something completely foolproof is to underestimate the ingenuity of complete fools.

Douglas Adams

Fewer companies actually make products these days than in the manufacturing heyday of years past. Today, the majority of the economy is driven by the twin engines of service and information. Yet, if you work in a manufacturing company, particularly one that markets products for consumers, design has never been more critical to your success. And it's never been more important to examine how you approach design and its corresponding effect on the behavior of your irrational customers.

Design with a Drinking Problem

We've all felt the power and influence of good—and bad—design on our emotions and behavior. I recall purchasing an "entry-level" luxury sedan a few years ago. Nice leather interior, all-wheel drive, responsive engine. Definitely a step up from my econo-Nissan. It was a "practical" decision ("it's safer than my old car!"), but even I inherently knew, at some level, I was simply rationalizing a much more emotional reason for the purchase ("I will look very cool in that sweet ride!"). Surely you've made similar purchases in the past, where you can't access your irrational subconscious to determine the real reason you "have to have" that flat-screen television, or $4,000 road bike, or embarrassingly expensive wrist watch, but you do know that it's not a totally rational decision.

My wife and I went to pick up the car at the dealership, stopping for a cup of coffee at Starbucks on the way. When we got to the showroom the car salesperson was there to shake my hand, and then meticulously and, yes, proudly even, run through the ins and outs of operating the gleaming new car. Finally, I was set loose. New-age key fob in hand, I plopped into the multiple-lumbar-supported electronically adjustable driver's seat and took a whiff of new-car smell. Anxious to get started, still clutching my Strarbucks Venti, I glanced to and fro, trying to locate the nearest cup holder. Then I tried to locate *any* cup holders. The sales person leaned in when he saw my confusion and hit a button in the center of the dash—near the stick shift, just below the multifunction Bose™ stereo. A small plastic ring glided out. I tentatively balanced my hot beverage in the holder, where it teetered precariously, seemingly in midair. With my first careful shift of gears, the cup shifted to one side, hot coffee spritzing up through the hole in the lid into the air, raining down on my hand (which had been resting on the gear shift), my pant leg, and the stereo.

After swearing, I started rethinking my choice in automobiles. With each turn, more coffee sloshed out into my previously pristine interior. A cup holder: It was something I hadn't even thought about as I shopped for cars. Such a simple thing. But apparently it was something the German engineers of my sedan hadn't given much thought either. Apparently, people in Germany don't sip coffee, or anything else, while they drive.

The car was my first choice, and I ended up adapting as best I could, but I never got over the irritation regarding the "lack-of-adequate-cup-holder" design. The design of products greatly impacts a customer's reaction—both at a conscious and subconscious level—and thus affects purchase choice and behavior. And there are a number of factors in the design of a product that really matter, both practically and emotionally, which is what we'll look at here.

Just What Is "Design"?

In order to discuss design and the most effective approaches to influencing the behavior of your irrational customers, we first have to consider just what we mean by the word. There are many definitions, but we're limiting our discussion to product design here. Still, even that narrowing of the conversation does little to clarify our focus. At its broadest, the concept of "design" applies to almost anything that's manufactured (or "created" like software and websites, which are not the focus of this chapter). Webster's Dictionary offers up this simple definition: "to create, fashion, execute, or construct according to plan." There are, of course several other definitions. Some take into account the "aesthetic, functional and other aspects" of a product (Wikipedia), but all have a common theme—that is, the idea of *intent* or *purpose*.

To design a product—and not just manufacture it—then, suggests a conscious effort to create something with intent, and with an eye toward the ultimate user. That's all well and good, but we need to dig a little deeper into the idea of design, and how one can develop products that resonate in a more fundamental sense with our customers.

Design That Touches the Human in All of Us

Surely there has been a product that you connected with on a deep, emotional level in your past. Perhaps a pocket knife, a table lamp, or a digital music player. When I was a boy, I had a baseball mitt that carried me through many summers. It was a Ted Williams autograph model, and I really loved that glove. I was a baseball nut, and spent countless hours playing catch with my best friend, playing in pickup games in the neighborhood, and in organized Little League games through the summer. The design of the mitt worked for me. It was incredibly functional, and it also just looked cool (at least to me). But there was something more. It wasn't just a tool I was using to be a better fielder; it was an extension of my hand, almost part of my body. I made sure that it was never left out in the backyard overnight, not just because it might waterlog the leather; I would feel guilty about it, and even feel bad for the mitt. Is it irrational to feel that way about a thing? Absolutely, but it's also powerful. As we'll see, if you can create products that elicit similar feelings, you're on the right track.

The Power of Anthropomorphic Design

In the early 1990s, Volkswagen reintroduced one of its former iconic products, the Volkswagen Beetle. Its design was reminiscent of the earlier versions from the 1950s, 1960s, and 1970s. The car was a smash, selling above and beyond expectations. Why was the newer iteration of the Beetle such a hit? When

Apple came out with the original Macintosh computer, it made a huge impact on the consumer marketplace. What was there about a personal computer that elicited such a strong, emotional response (and continues to do so decades later) with its intensely loyal customer base? The answer lies in how we subconsciously react to human traits in product design.

Anthropomorphism is a concept that, at its most basic, means "like a human." We are hard-wired to respond to human elements or traits, especially faces. In fact, infants at very early stages of development possess the ability to recognize specific faces. In his book *Emotional Design*,[1] Donald Norman, a cognitive scientist, explains that we are all biologically set up to socially interact with others, in part by identifying their emotions (is somebody smiling or frowning?). Anthropomorphism is this innate tendency we possess to apply emotions and characteristics to not just other people but also to animals, and, if given the chance, inanimate objects. Note that we *subconsciously* apply these characteristics to things; it's not a conscious choice on our part.

This trait of ours applies to not just the physical appearance of things, but also the social and psychological characteristics of products. So, for instance, if you own an object that makes your life easier, like a PC or cell phone, or just better in some way, like my beloved baseball mitt, you instinctively attribute human tendencies or traits to it. The product becomes more than a "thing," even if you consciously understand that's exactly what it is. Yet we can't help ourselves; our more powerful subconscious makes the call, and as a result, the "thing" becomes a friend.

The Human Bias of the Irrational Subconscious

Why do we have this anthropomorphic trait in the first place? What purpose does it serve to subconsciously apply human traits to animals and inanimate objects? As stated in David Linden's

The Accidental Mind and other recent books on how our brains evolved, it's really a question of survival. As our brains developed through the ages, starting at the brain stem (in charge of many basic subconscious functions) and moving forward toward the more sophisticated processing areas of the brain, one of the keys to surviving through another day rested in our ability to identify another person as friend or foe. What were the intentions of a person who was approaching? Thus, we developed "fast-twitch" mental muscles in the more powerful, subconscious part of the brain. It's the ability to first quickly identify a specific face (family or stranger?) and then determine a person's intent by his or her facial expression. (Smile? Give her a hug? Frown? Throw a rock at him and run?) It's in part these fast-twitch muscles that create this strong reaction to more "human" forms, whether animate or not.

In addition, we are, inherently, social animals. We rely on and require interaction with others. All people are programmed to connect with other people. It's another survival trait. As we evolved, humans gained intelligence and adaptability through the development of our larger, more powerful brains, as well as the ability to work in groups to better ensure the safety and well being of each member of the group. At the same time, we lost some of our natural defenses to predators and the elements, like less body hair and reduced agility (for climbing trees, for instance). These human traits, David Linden and others argue, which developed in the distant past as our brains evolved, have not gone away. We're still driven by many of these subconscious forces in our behavior today.

Irrational Design Is More Effective Design

In their paper *From Seduction to Fulfillment: The Use of Anthropomorphic Form in Design*,[2] authors Carl DiSalvo and Francine

Gemperie state that it's generally accepted "though rarely written about," that the front grills of most automobiles are designed to resemble faces. Think about it the next time you're driving and look in the rear view mirror. The Volkswagen Beetle looks friendly and nonthreatening, in contrast to the aggressive "face" of a Hummer. Is it better to be friendly or aggressive? It depends on the consumer, of course. Subconsciously, a driver might want to feel powerful, like he or she is in charge and strong—a feeling reinforced in the grill of the Hummer. Another car buyer, a person perhaps who seeks a social connection with others, may identify with the amiable face of the Beetle. Observing reactions to visual stimuli (i.e., observing how people react to something, not asking them), and utilizing metaphors to do a "deeper dive" on research are just two methods for developing the right "faces" for the target markets.

While the science regarding anthropomorphic design is relatively recent, the concept has been around for quite a while. We could go back centuries to carved representations of gods, but let's start a century or so in the past. In their article mentioned above, the authors DiSalvo and Gemperie use the example of perfume bottles that represents the curves of a woman's torso as eliciting a strong emotional (and yes, irrational subconscious) response. The connection is important, between the product itself and a package design that represents the product's property or benefits (sensuality for perfume; aggression for a Hummer).

Does the soft curve of a perfume bottle or the snarling "face" of a Hummer grill make the product any better or worse? Not necessarily. Many aspects of design are directly related to the functionality of a product, obviously a critical factor. To oversimplify an example: the finger-hole placement and the overall shape of a bowling ball. Obviously, any other shape would seem to be to the detriment of the product's intended purpose. But what about the feel of your cell phone, the size of the lapels on your suit coat, or the shape of your wine glasses? Yes, some of it could be argued to be engineering, but often great design involves tapping into the irrational subconscious, to use design at the more emotional level. Eric Du Plessis, in *The Advertised Mind*, argues that emotions are what drive decisions. And prolific author on graphic design Steven Heller, in the *AIGA Journal of Design*,[3] says, "There is hardly a single designed object—from automobile to ziggurat—that does not have an emotional root." Create strong emotions—ideally positive ones—and you can drive customer behavior.

By creating products that are anthropomorphic in some respect—physically, socially, or psychologically—you are improving the odds that you will elicit an emotional response, and that in turn increases the likelihood that you will drive customer behavior.

Patterns and Your Irrational Subconscious

Much of our thinking is done in the subconscious, the irrational part of our brain. One of the ways the subconscious helps us get through the world each day is by identifying patterns. As we're confronted with a situation, a choice, or a product, our brain automatically scans and identifies patterns that we've encountered in the past. It's this ability to identify these patterns that allows us to do things while on "automatic pilot."

So, for example, when you want to enjoy a cold beverage at a friend's house while watching the football game, you walk over to the refrigerator and pull the door open without thinking about it. The pattern has been established, in your subconscious over many years and thousands of uses, that a refrigerator door pulls open. It doesn't push open; it doesn't slide to the side. It's a pattern that you don't think about, but it's there, and there's a chance that if it's disrupted you will experience frustration. I know this seems like an absurd example, but the point remains that no matter what type of product you are selling, chances are over time your customers, at a subconscious level, will have built up certain expectations for what the product is and how it will be used.

Given that, as you approach the design of your products, a delicate balance must be achieved. You must be innovative and stay out ahead of your competition, creating desirable products that resonate emotionally with your customers. But at the same time, you must temper that with a knowledge of the fundamental usability, texture, colors, etc. that are core to the customer's expectations for your products. It's absolutely possible to change those subconscious patterns with your customers, but it's not easy. After all, if you get so innovative that you are far out in front of your customers' ability to reconcile the new product with the existing patterns within their subconscious, your design could backfire. The trick is to innovate in ways that improve your product but don't shock the customer's expectations.

Testing Your Designs: It's *Still* About Behavior

While discussing customer research, in Chapter 6 and elsewhere, I suggested that the only way to get at what customers are really thinking in their irrational subconscious was to focus not on what they said, but rather on what they did. It's the customers' behavior that uncovers "the truth," that gives you a peek into that inaccessible area of the irrational subconscious. The challenge with product design in particular is determining just how one might approach accomplishing that.

One strong lesson we've learned is not to engage in "design by focus group." It doesn't work. Customer opinions matter, but customers aren't designers. Instead, look to companies like Bang & Olufsen, the well-regarded, high-end electronics manufacturer. It puts all its faith in a small group of key designers, to the point where a designer can halt the manufacture of a cell phone or mp3 player if it's a millimeter too thick or the screen is a hair too small. They know their customers (and the company brand promise) better, in most cases, than the customers know themselves. The results are an occasional miscalculation, but otherwise an admirable product and financial track record.

Another example is Apple. Steve Jobs has, on numerous occasions, discussed his view of the importance of design, as well as the appropriate approach to it: "It's really hard to design products by focus groups. A lot of times, people don't know what they want until you show it to them."[4] Apple, like Bang & Olufsen, approaches design by understanding its customers. Jobs also said, "You can't just ask customers what they want and then try to give it to them. By the time you get it built, they'll want something new."

Steve Jobs is, as you may know, an evangelist about product design. He sees the power of design as being the distinct advantage of Apple, and as a result, design is incorporated into all aspects of the Apple customer experience, from the products to the stores, to the websites, and even to the product documentation. In Jobs's opinion (which dictates Apple's philosophy, given his authority), the goal with product design is not to hit "singles and doubles," but rather "home runs" with Apple products. And it's clear that, to accomplish this, you don't do surveys and focus groups. The "proof is in the pudding" with Apple and, given the success of the Macintosh, the iPod, and the iPhone, it's hard to argue with the approach.

Let me reach back for one more famous example of the power of design without the need to ask for customer input. In the mid-1980s, Sony was trying to create a new personal CD player, similar to what it had accomplished earlier with its Walk-man cassette player. The head of the "General Audio Division" of Sony, Kozo Ohsone, sat down with his design group and held up a piece of wood that was about 13 centimeters across and 4 centimeters thick. "Make it this size." He knew Sony's customers. Based on the success of the Walkman, he under-stood that the CD player needed to be a certain size and shape that would be easy to carry to be a success. They made the tech-nology work within the dimensions of that block of wood, and the company had another success story. It's not about focus groups. In a way, it demonstrates the power of empathy—the ability to walk in the shoes of your customers.

They Want It All . . . Until They Don't

There's another concept, related to the irrational subconscious, that's important to keep in mind when approaching product design. It's the idea that customers, if given the chance to pro-vide input into the design of a product, have a tendency to "overshoot," so to speak, and ask for the world, when all they really want is something that works well. Let me elaborate.

In a recent study cited by Jame Surowiecki,[5] participants had a chance to design a new cell phone with the bells and whistles they thought they desired. Each participant was pre-sented with a list of thirty possible features on his or her cell phone model. It was a classic example of how some companies approach design: Ask your customers. And what do you think the customers selected? The camera feature? Of course! GPS? Sure! And what about the other features? For the most part, the participants selected ALL the features. Almost every customer was looking for a cell phone that was absolutely laden down with features. This tendency of customers extended into the store as well: When given the choice of a simple phone with a few features or a "robo-phone" that can do a plethora of things, most customers select the multifeatured cell phone.

Now here's the interesting part: When asked, after using the feature-heavy cell phones, about their happiness with the product, most respondents were not thrilled. So customers claim they want a bunch of features built into their phones, they buy those phones when presented with an array of choices, and yet are ultimately unhappy after using the phones for a few months. What's going on?

This hearkens back to an earlier point about the irrational customer. We all have a hard time projecting how we will feel about some product or circumstance in the future. The problem is that we are incapable of understanding how the context of the situation will influence our feelings. It's a concept we visited earlier, called focalism. Consequently, it's hard to trust any customer when asking what he or she wants in the future. In this case, the idea of a phone that does everything was extremely appealing in theory. But the reality is, once customers had the phone in their pockets and purses and went about living their lives, they found that they used only a few of the available features, and that the additional features, simply added complexity to the everyday functioning of the phone.

Once again, the answer to understanding how to design your products in a way that customers appreciate is behavior. Don't trust your customers to tell you what they want. They're incapable. Better to observe actual behavior whenever possible. Ideally, like at Bang & Olufsen, you design based on innovation and creativity of your designers, and then validate the new products. There are several ways to do this.

One is to take Procter and Gamble's approach. Procter and Gamble is a consumer product behemoth, a fixture in the American business landscape for the last hundred years. The company, more than most, understands the dynamics of the consumer marketplace, and the importance of learning customer preferences through observation of customer behavior. P&G regularly sends its product managers out in the field to people's homes to observe how customers use their products in real time. By direct observation of a customer washing dishes, brushing her teeth, changing diapers, etc., they gain a perspective on how the customer perceives P&G products, and they see the pleasure or the frustration that comes with everyday use of its soaps, shampoos, food items, and detergents. They can then take this information back to improve the next version of those products. It's through direct observation of the customers that a company can get a better handle on the truth.

Another approach is to bring customers to you, allowing them to interact with current and new products. Your company invites customers in to observe how they interact with the product. It's not ideal, as the environment does matter for understanding the context within which customers use the product, but it's far superior to simply talking to your customers about size, shape, feel, and functionality.

At its simplest, what I'm saying is, "Watch your customers using your products." Approaching product design with some understanding of your irrational customers can give you a powerful advantage over your competition. Ignoring how customers really behave with your products, versus just what they say about your products, can be a dangerous proposition.

So . . . What Do I Do Now?

Competent product design is about function at its most basic; it's an engineering exercise. But to connect with and retain your customers at a more powerful, emotional level, you must journey beyond just engineering to a more transcendent design plane. You have an opportunity, through innovative, anthropomorphic design, to create products that elicit positive feelings in the irrational subconscious of your customers. It takes a more thoughtful approach, but as you can see in some of our examples, the results are worth the extra effort.

1. *Don't Ask Your Customers What They Want.* As we've seen, recent research demonstrates that we are all very poor at articulating how we feel about the present situation. And we're even worse at understanding or articulating how we might feel about a product or situation in the future. Yet companies continue to conduct focus groups and surveys that will provide, at best, less-than-accurate information. So, yes, I know this is a negative in the "What Do I Do Now?" category, but it's important: Don't just ask your customers what they want, because they are incapable of telling you. Rather, test your ideas with prototypes and, if possible, in real-world situations.

2. *Encourage Innovation from Your Designers.* Some of the best consumer product companies, like Apple and Bang & Olufsen, rely on a core group of innovative designers. The companies trust that the designers can "walk in the customers' shoes" to understand their wants and needs and develop products that customers will ultimately demand, but may not be able to yet envision or request. While there may be the occasional "strike," there's also a higher likelihood that you'll hit a "home run."

3. *Exploit (and Don't Violate) Our Subconscious Expectations.* To drive a car, you don't use a joystick, you use a steering wheel. You turn the wheel right, and the car moves right, turn the wheel left and the car goes left. It's great to be in-

novative, to push the envelope in terms of what your product can do for customers, but that must be tempered by the subconscious patterns of expectation and usage already residing in your customers.

4. *Focus on Customer Behavior.* Throughout this book, I've preached that "behavior is truth." Only through observing the customer interacting with your product can you start to understand just how effective your design has been. It's as simple as "watch the customer use your product." Do this, and you'll be far ahead of the typical business.

Chapter 10

Irrational Employees: Hire for Emotion; Train for Skills

I rate enthusiasm even above professional skill.

Edward Appleton

This book is about your customers: how they are irrational, and what you can do to better understand and interact with them. So far we've talked about the irrational subconscious, what it is and how it is inaccessible to the conscious mind, as well as how it processes up to 95 percent of the cognitive activity happening at any moment. We've also discussed how your customers are not very good at telling you how they feel and even worse at projecting what they might do in the future. Plus, we've explored some of the things you can do to better understand your customers, given the quirkiness of how they think, and what you might do to better drive a desired behavior.

One of the major factors in delivering the right products and service to your irrational customers is hiring employees with the natural ability to connect with them on an emotional level. In order to do so, you must look at your employees and determine just what makes them tick.

Well, I've got news for you: Employees are irrational too.

If you are irrational (and you are), it holds that your employees are irrational as well. The way they take in and process the world around them, and the way the irrational subconscious identifies patterns and helps make decisions (typically without much help from the conscious portion of the brain) is identical to what we've described in terms of your customers. Because we are all customers of one company or another, and many of us are employees, it follows that much of what works with customers will also work with the irrational human beings who work for your company. While the desired behavior for employees might be different from the behavior you hope to evoke from your customers, it no doubt involves creating the emotions that drive a desired behavior.

So we need to look at the type of behavior you're hoping for from your employees and then examine how some companies have been successful in finding employees to connect in that irrational, emotional way with customers. There are companies who know what they want from their employees and have figured out how to recruit employees that naturally possess inherent attributes that result in the desired behavior, as well as how to create incentives and training that will achieve a desirable result through your employees. Let's look at a few examples and explore just what you can do to create an irrational, potent workforce that resonates with your irrational customers.

Finding the Right People

While working for a large insurance company years ago, I, like every employee there, suffered through what we came to label as the "flavor of the month" company initiatives. One initiative would be introduced with great fanfare every six months or so: "Quality," "Six Sigma," "Reengineering," and so on. During one of these "paradigm shifting" efforts, a phrase emerged that became ubiquitous in the hallways and meeting rooms of the home office: "It's not the people, it's the process." Although this was a hard concept for many of us to swallow, I don't want to discount the importance of process in a company's performance (in fact, we'll be focusing on it in the next chapter). But the conclusion and catchphrase most employees in any company would naturally come to over time is: "It's absolutely about the people." Some companies get this, and some don't. Here's one that does.

Hiring for Emotion

Danny Meyer is the founder of Union Square Hospitality Group—a very successful group of restaurants in New York City—and the author of *Setting the Table*,[1] an interesting account of just how a Midwestern kid from St. Louis became the king of the New York restaurant scene. In the book, Meyer revisits his victories and his failures on the way to starting his first restaurant, the Union Square Café, an oasis steps off Union Square in the middle of Manhattan. It went on to be awarded Zagat Survey's New York City's Favorite Restaurant for seven straight years. Meyer and his team have gone on to create a number of other unique restaurants throughout New York and in 2008 in Las Vegas as well.

My wife and I dined at Union Square Café on a trip to the city several years ago. I made the reservation with some trepidation, as I figured (knowing New York) any place with such notoriety would be very crowded, and probably very expensive. We were almost shocked, by contrast, with the actual experience. Yes, the food was excellent, and the layout and feel of the restaurant were comfortable. But what made the experience superior was how we were treated. It wasn't the rushed, hectic feel of other popular NYC eateries. The best way I can put it is that it was a compelling combination of everyone, from hostess to our waiter, being welcoming and real. I actually thought they were happy to see us and that it mattered to them whether we had a nice dinner. Of course, they were all, it appeared, technically skilled at their jobs, but there was more to it. They were genuine.

The waiter was friendly and conversational, unlike some of the haughtier folks I've encountered at fine restaurants in New York and elsewhere. Meyer bases his entire philosophy of success around one central idea: "enlightened hospitality," and when you go to one of his restaurants it shows. Visits to some of his other restaurants in the city, including Tabla (with Indian-influenced cuisine) and Shake Shack, a walk-up retro shake and hamburger joint in the middle of Madison Square Park downtown, as well as on the Upper West Side, are very different experiences, but deliver a consistent and friendly vibe through empathetic and enthusiastic employees. Surely the answer isn't just to train employees to "be nice."

I wondered exactly how Danny Meyer pulled off this unique feat of finding people (in New York no less!) who excelled in the specific skills requisite to their positions, but who also seemed to possess an inherent attitude, a natural predisposition, to being—for lack of a better word—"nice." In his book, Meyer elaborates on his philosophy. In short, he hires for emotional intelligence over technical competency. He feels it's essential that the employee start with a certain attitude, an optimism toward life, and an inherent drive to help other people, not just in their jobs, but in their day-to-day lives.

Weigh Employees on an Emotional Intelligence Scale

Meyer calls these engaged employees "51 percenters," a term coined by one of Meyer's mentors, Chicago restaurateur Rich Melman. Meyer describes 51 percenters as possessing five key traits: warmth and optimism, a natural intelligence and curiosity, a strong work ethic, empathy, and self-awareness. Of course, he's always looking for the right technical skill sets in new hires, but more importantly (i.e., of 51 percent importance) is the right set of inherent emotional skills. By employing people with these behavioral traits (with, as Meyer puts it, "a dazzling sparkle in the eye"), he can be confident that they will fulfill his mission of providing a unique form of "enlightened hospitality" (which Meyer clearly differentiates from other service aspirations) to his customers. The phenomenal success of his restaurants is compelling evidence that he's on the right track.

Do you look for "51 percenters" when you hire new employees? Can you find employees who, at their very core, have the attitude to excel in their relationships with your customers? If you can succeed in recruiting that type of person, regardless of your processes and training programs, you're more than halfway home. You have people who, within their deep, inaccessible subconscious, start with optimism, warmth, and empathy, who will naturally seek to "do the right thing." Think of the value to customer interactions when that is the foundation.

It's Not "How Do They Think?" It's "How Do They Act?"

You might agree, in principle, that it would be great indeed to find these positive, upbeat, helpful employees, especially for your frontline positions. But the trick is determining who is really a "51 percenter." One thing we already know: Just asking people about their approach, feelings, or philosophy won't do you a lot of good. A job candidate can do one of three things when asked about personal attitudes or feelings toward serving customers: (1) He can lie and, after all, many of us can be tempted to fib a little in an interview if we think it might paint us in a better light. (2) She can tell you what she thinks is the truth, and be wrong, since, as we've seen, we cannot directly access the irrational subconscious. It's the subconscious that determines our emotions, and as a result, how we ultimately behave. Or (3) he can tell the truth, and be right. You might get lucky, and the candidate can, effectively, guess at deep-seated feelings and attitudes and be right. But do you want to take that chance? There are some other ways to get a clearer picture about a candidate's attitude and emotional investment in the job.

Past Behavior Equals Future Behavior

One thing we've learned, especially when searching for client- or customer-facing employees, is to approach the evaluation of a job candidate with an eye toward behavior. Behavior is truth, and it serves you well to more carefully examine a candidate's past behavior before getting into the interview. By examining performance in previous positions, you can spot tendencies that would not otherwise come out but that can give you insight into how he or she might approach the new position.

How do you do this? The best way is to make phone calls to references provided (and if the candidate has trouble providing a few, it's a red flag) to find out what the candidate actually did (behavior) in those jobs. Many past employers, when called, are reluctant to disclose much about an employee's past performance. They may say they can only confirm dates of employment and title. But try anyway. If a candidate was really excellent—or really horrible—in a previous position, the employer will often find a way to tell you if given a chance. Does this seem overly simplistic? Maybe, but think of your last few hires. If you're like many employers, you didn't do your due diligence on the candidate's past performance. And that often leads to poor fits in your company.

The Interview: Focus on Behavior

All right, you can do your best to determine past behavior through references and referrals, and you have another opportunity to get at, not just technical competency but attitude, in the interview. There are two ways to do this. First: observe. The idea is to use the interview to put the employee in a predefined situation, then observe the behavior.

There's an old sketch from Monty Python, the outrageous British comedy troupe of the 1970s, where John Cleese conducts a hilarious interview with a befuddled job candidate. In the skit, Cleese suddenly starts yelling out a countdown, "Five! Four! Three! Two! One!" The candidate, of course, doesn't know what to do, and Cleese says "interesting" and makes a note. Then he starts ringing a bell arbitrarily, again observing the increasingly desperate candidate, and makes another note. The skit is funny and pure nonsense, but in a way, it is not dissimilar to what I'm suggesting you do in your interviews.

Here's something we've done at Vox: The interview is scheduled for, let's say 2:00. He or she might be under the impression it's with just one of our managers. However, when the candidate arrives, he's asked to wait for a few minutes in the reception area. Our receptionist notes the candidate's behavior. Is she impatient, smiling, checking her watch, making calls on her cell phone?

Once the candidate is shown into a room, he is confronted with not one manager, but two or three. It's the job of one of the Vox employees to simply observe the candidate's behavior throughout the interview and take notes. We observe his body language, which has been shown to provide insights into the real feelings of a person. Someone who sits back with his or her arms crossed, for instance, is typically insecure or uncomfortable. We watch for reactions to some of the interview questions. Does she get defensive, does she laugh often, look us in the eyes?

Of course, beyond observing, the interview is for asking the candidate questions. This is the area many companies fall down on—the questions themselves. Too many managers or HR folks approach the interview as a casual discussion. The key again is behavior. It's not asking, "How do you feel about . . ." or "Did you get along well with others in your previous position?" Rather, the questions must be focused on behavior. Zero in on specific examples. By forcing the candidate to dig into individual instances or illustrations from past performance, you get to the meat of who this person is. Questions we use include: "Can you tell us about a specific time that you were interacting with a really difficult person who didn't agree with you about a solution or recommendation? How did you come to some resolution?" A question like this can illuminate how the candidate is likely to behave in the future, as it's based on past behavior.

Test for Behavior

Do you sense a theme here? Yes, it's great to hear what a prospective employee has to say, and you can get closer to the truth about attitude and future behavior by strategically interviewing him or her with behavior-based questions, but there's another way to seek a "window" into the irrational subconscious, to help you determine the engagement of a prospective employee—by testing.

There are a variety of cognitive and personality tests available, from ink blots to the Myers-Briggs Type Indicator, and they have become more popular in recent years. A recent study by the American Management Association reports that 39 percent of those surveyed used some type of personality test for hiring purposes. One that we use regularly at Vox is called "DISC" Assessment. The letters in "DISC" refer to the four personality tendencies that any individual might possess, with some being more prominent than others within each individual. The "D" stands for "dominance," which includes people who are goal oriented, with little patience for rules or process. Many CEOs are "Ds." "I" stands for "influence." These people are more social, and seek acceptance and recognition from others (as opposed to the "Ds"). Some "Is" make great salespeople, and are also well suited for customer-facing roles. "S" stands for "steadiness." In short, these are good team players. They enjoy working with others toward a common goal. Finally, there is "C," which stands for "conscientious." A "C" is a detail-oriented person, someone who prefers to understand the rules and steps before setting to work, but then does an outstanding job.

We like this tool for looking at behavioral styles and preferences. It's a good way to see which behavioral traits are strongest in an individual, which can help us project just how an individual might best fit into a particular role. Be careful, however, with putting too much weight into tools such as these. While we all share some common tendencies, none of us are all one thing or another. Rather we are each an olio, if you will, a mix of behavioral traits and tendencies. But understanding these inherent tendencies has real value. For instance, for customer-facing positions, a person who, on DISC evaluation, registers high on "C" (conscientious, needs to know rules and processes) but low on "I" (influencer, a "people person") may not be a perfect fit.

The Final Test: Ask Them to Quit!

Most companies are happy these days to recruit competent employees without worrying too much about their level of engagement. Sure, you want employees who are happy to be there, and who do their jobs well, but is that enough?

As far as Zappos, the online shoe retailer we mentioned in Chapter 9, is concerned, the answer is absolutely not. When Zappos hires an employee, it puts him or her through an intense four-week training process, which involves sitting in on and then directly handling customer calls and more. Throughout the training the employee receives a full salary. But Zappos is committed to not just recruiting employees who can "do the job," but those who are truly committed and emotionally engaged. So at the end of the training period, the company makes the employee an offer: If you quit right now, you get a check for $2,000. $2,000!

Think about this as a strategy. It seems to cut against typical business logic. You spend money for recruiting and money for hiring what appears to be a qualified candidate. Then you pay the employee's full salary for the first month, and you spend more to ensure that the employee is properly trained. And then, when the employee is set to become truly productive, you offer him or her $2,000 . . . to quit! It's downright irrational! And yet, for Zappos, it makes perfect sense. They've established that customer service is their *raison d'etre*. Their business lives and dies by the quality of the relationship it establishes between its frontline employees and its customers. They've found that an employee who is capable and properly trained, but who is not properly engaged, cannot create a compelling, emotional relationship with the customer. In that respect, the $2,000 is not seen as an expense by the company; rather, it's an investment in their philosophy and their business model.

What Zappos has found is that the majority of new employees pass on the $2,000. Those who remain are invested in the company's success and have proven that they gain satisfaction not just from monetary rewards, but more from the recognition and inherent fulfillment from doing their jobs—which at Zappos means thrilling customers—extremely well. And when you are staffed with this type of employee, as a company you can increase the level of freedom and empowerment the employee has in day-to-day business situations.

Employee Engagement

Companies spend millions each year on employee communications that attempt to drive a desired behavior in their employees. We have been involved in a number of large-scale communications efforts designed to get the client's field staff to think like the home office staff, or to convince agents or brokers to sell more products, or to get frontline employees to think about interactions from the customer's perspective.

But if you are not talking to engaged employees, all your attempts to encourage a certain type of behavior could be for naught. Engaged employees are, in fact, the secret to long-term success for many companies. Here's what I mean by "engaged" employees—employees who are invested in the company's success, not just because it might mean a bonus or some tangible reward, but rather because they feel as though they are working for a cause or mission that is inherently fulfilling. Engaged employees are not constantly looking for the rational rewards like compensation. At Vox, our greater cause is to help make life a little easier or more pleasant for our clients' customers. Of course, paying your people a competitive wage is important, but studies have shown that's not what drives your great employees.

An Employment "Containment" Strategy

An "engaged employee equals higher customer retention" approach is also taken at the Container Store. Founders Kip Tindell and Garrett Boone have always implicitly known that by treating employees with care and respect (and more money), they would make a healthy return on their investment. So they pay more, train more, and provide lifestyle flexibility. If you walk into a Container Store, you'll notice several things right away: More people seem to be working and roaming the floor compared to other stores, and those people are universally good natured and helpful. The store gains engagement and loyalty by providing flexibility for the lifestyle needs of its employees. For instance, many of their employees are parents who need to be home before and after school for their kids. The result is engaged employees who, in turn, treat customers with care and respect.

The other benefit to companies who actively work to engage their employees is higher retention. Let's take another look at Maslow's hierarchy of needs. Many companies are complacent in terms of meeting the emotional needs of their employees, sticking with the first two levels of the pyramid—physiological and safety. Companies like the Container Store, however, understand that appealing to the higher levels of emotional needs—needs like esteem and self-actualization—with their employees can create a deeper connection between the employee and the company and customers.

There is no perfect "how-to" guide to creating fully engaged employees. A company must commit to that ideal for it to become a reality. The challenge is that it's not just about salary levels, or vacation policies, or working conditions, or career tracks, or training. It's all that and more. It's a sincere commitment to create a company where great people want to work, a company that has a real vision for what it wants to be. We'll look at some specifics that can start a company down this road.

Emotional Engagement as a Business Strategy

Engaged employees are really the first, and probably most important, step to a great irrational customer experience. Great products and solid processes help, but without employees who are invested in the customer's well-being, the company risks creating negative emotions. And financially, dedicated, caring employees translate to lower overall expenses due to industry-low employee turnover, combined with consistent revenue growth and higher profits. Research by Gallup and others has consistently shown a strong correlation between the level of employee engagement at a company and financial results.

Take a look at Best Buy. While most companies—particularly retail companies—live and die by the hardcore financial numbers (same store sales, for instance), Best Buy leans on an additional metric to predict success for its individual locations. Like many other retailers, its business challenges include harnessing and directing the energy of a workforce that includes many part-time and student-age employees. It's a daunting task, but Best Buy found that, by focusing on employee empowerment and engagement, it could drive the store performance.

It creates engaged employees by, in part, allowing these part-time young people to have a say in how their individual stores are run. Best Buy allows a maximum amount of flexibility in how employees schedule their time and look to the store's workers to connect emotionally with the store's customers through training on customer "personas." For example, young urban males are nicknamed "Buzz." Upper middle class women are called "Jill." As Darren Jackson, the company's Chief Financial Officer has said regarding the importance of employee engagement, ". . . we find that when employee engagement is up, so is our profitability, so is our customer satisfaction, so is our bottom line."[2]

Walk in the Employee's Shoes

When you think about it, your employees, in many ways, are just like your customers. They think like customers, they want the same things as your customers—to belong to an organization that fits in with their life story. And you want much of the same thing from your employees as your customers, in that you want them to be loyal to the company, to stay with your business.

What else can you do, then, to better understand your irrational employees, to gain insight on what makes them tick so that you can design the employee experience in a way that attracts and retains your most valuable employees? Ultimately, it's about empathy. Specifically for frontline employees, you must walk in their shoes.

How do you do that? Some companies have programs that require executives to move through the frontline areas of the organization, observing exactly how those valuable employees are doing their jobs. But even if your company doesn't have a formal program to allow that type of exposure, you need to find a way to see and hear firsthand just what is happening on the frontline. By talking directly with the employees who are in turn dealing directly with your irrational customers, you'll get the exposure you need to the tools they use, their processes, and their attitudes. What you may find is that the reality for these soldiers is dramatically different from the assumptions being made in the executive suites.

At the same time, by approaching your frontline employees with the same goals and same perspective that you have with your customer (i.e., that they are irrational and subject to the same motivations, fears, etc.), you can gain a better understanding of their situations and develop strategies and tools that can help them perform at a high level.

The Other Benefit of Understanding Your Frontline Employees: A Better Customer Experience

You've gone to the trouble of walking in your employees' shoes to understand their experience. This helps you to better shape the employee experience by addressing their deeper, irrational and emotional needs, like belonging and recognition. But there's an additional, tremendous benefit beyond a group of engaged employees. By understanding your frontline employees, you also begin to better understand those interactions and communications they have with your customers.

Think of the possibilities. By simply employing empathy as a strategy with your employees, you will put yourself in your frontline employees' shoes and gain insight into their best ideas regarding the customer experience. Remember, our overall goal is to create a compelling experience for your irrational customers.

With your frontline employees allowing you a window into that experience, you possess a tremendous advantage over your competition regarding customer service.

So . . . What Do I Do Now?

Your employees and their interactions with your customers are critical for understanding and driving desired behavior from your irrational customers. To do that, you must find and keep emotionally intelligent customers.

1. *To Hire for Emotional Intelligence, Look at Behavior.* Your goal, just like Danny Meyer's, should be to hire for emotional intelligence, and then train for skills. But just like irrational customers, you can't trust everything job candidates say, not because they are trying to mislead you, but because they can't access their irrational subconscious. As we've seen, behavior is the truth. Do your due diligence on past performance. Talk to previous employers about what the candidate did. Observe the candidate during the interview. And when you are asking the interviewees questions, make sure they focus on behavior and not just attitudes and opinions. Finally, take a page from Zappos and create a situation where the candidate's *behavior* will determine his or her fit at your company.

2. *Engage and Then Empower Your Employees.* Of course, most employees will say that they are motivated by money, but that's not necessarily the case. Just like your customers, you must discover what resonates with your employees. Is it a sense of mission? Is it belonging to a special group of people, or gaining recognition? There's no engaging with-

out some form of empowerment. But if you have the right employees, this gets much easier.

3. *Walk in Your Employees' Shoes.* You need to put your front-line employees in a position to succeed in their interactions with your customers. You can't do that unless you know exactly what they're going through each day. But in most companies, that just doesn't happen. Preach and practice empathetic management. Physically get in the frontline employee's space and walk through what he or she does every day. By gaining a full understanding of the employee's situation, you also gain insights into the customer experience, and you can create the role that sparks engagement and challenges in your best employees.

Chapter 11

Process This: Tying It All Together

A complex system that works is invariably found to have evolved from a simple system that works.

John Gaule

Products must be designed and produced. Services must be offered. Websites need to be created. Employees have to be hired and trained. And your customers must be accommodated. On their own, however, all of these things are not sufficient to create a cohesive experience for your irrational customers. In order for your company to create a compelling connection and a positive perception with your customers, you must also look at the final inherent element of the customer experience—process.

Let me be clear about what I mean by *customer process*. A customer process is any procedure or system that directly impacts the customer, but its benefit can be twofold. It can be a process initiated or conducted by the company, like a system for when and how it sends out customer invoices, or a process that the customer must navigate, such as a sales transaction on the company website.

What I've personally experienced, seen with our clients, and also heard from others in a variety of corporations, is that many processes designed to serve customers not only don't create optimal interactions, but often get in the way of any authentic, quality experience. Of course, a customer's feelings and behavior are dictated by the activity in the irrational subconscious, but it's not just the *what*—the product design, the customer letters, the call center scripts—it's the *how* that dictates whether customers will jump on board, buy your products, use your services, and stay with your company.

Why Process Is Important

Think of almost any industry you might deal with as a customer and you'll begin to understand why it's critical that businesses create and maintain processes that produce a positive perception for their customers. For instance, consider the airline industry. Is the process of boarding a plane the same for each airline? For some maybe, but not all. Anyone who flies Southwest knows that its process is based on lining up in a certain way in order to get on the plane, but that there aren't assigned seats, which is significantly different than the way other major carriers handle boarding. Is that process better or worse for customers? That depends on the customer and what his or her expectations are. But regardless, it's a thoughtful, conscious process that the company created, which is what I'm suggesting you do for any of your "customer-facing" processes.

Or consider the two restaurants mentioned in the Introduction. Was the customer process an important factor for customers? At Little Louie's, the process involved pushing through a crowd as best you could to a wooden counter in a hot, noisy room and yelling out your order. At the other more exclusive and expensive restaurant, the process was effortless: being attended to by a solicitous waiter, who happily accepted your order and soon brought you your selected delicacies while you relaxed in a tranquil environment. Is one process better than the other? It depends! It depends on your brand promise, the customers' expectations, and more.

The key here is that the process is purposeful, that it's creating an intentional customer experience, and not just the result of selfish internal goals like company efficiencies or employee convenience.

The Unintended Impact of Inadvertent Processes

Years ago, when I was in charge of customer communications at a major insurance company, we were responsible for the content of literally millions of letters, statements, and notices sent out to customers each month. Given the volume, process was an important element in assuring that customers received the right message at the right time. But sometimes we inadvertently created problems with customers, not because of *what* we told them, but *when* we told it to them. Let me give you an example.

One profitable customer, who carried both homeowners and auto insurance policies with us and had been with the company for at least ten years, received one of our customer letters that congratulated him on both his safe driving and his company loyalty. But there was another process occurring at the same time. A separate letter was generated and sent to the same customer concerning the inspection of the exterior of his home. The result of these two independent processes was that, just a day or two after congratulating this long-time client on being one of our most desirable customers, we essentially threatened him with a message that said, in so many words, "fix your porch or we will cancel your homeowners insurance." Needless to say, the customer was not pleased. It was like we were patting him on the back with one hand and punching him in the gut with the other.

This wasn't a communications problem; this was a process problem. It was an instance where a process left a customer with both a negative impression and with negative emotions. And as we all know, emotions drive behavior.

Process exists in all companies to a greater or lesser degree. Even when a company doesn't purposely design a process, often a *de facto* process "emerges," like magic, to fill a void. Regardless of how it's created, it can be a necessary evil or a customer benefit, depending on the situation. For you, in your company, the challenge will be to figure out which process is which.

Your customers, as we have discussed throughout the book, are irrational. They develop emotions based on experiences with your company. These emotions are created in the irrational subconscious, which in turn drives their behavior. Just like the other aspects of customer experience we've examined, from the design of the website to the tone of the customer service representative's voice in the call center, to the wording on a brochure, the existence and quality level of key customer processes are critical for company success.

The Danger of Too Little Process . . .

So, process is necessary. Without it, as you've no doubt experienced in your own company, things tend to "slip through the cracks." Companies with too little process regarding customer service allow mistakes to occur without ever realizing it. By simply making assumptions that the right things will just happen on their own, these companies put frontline employees in a difficult position. Without the tools and the process to back them up, even these employees grow disillusioned. Your excellent employees (the "51 percenters," as Danny Meyer calls them) will do everything possible to still create a quality customer experience, but eventually get worn down. At the same time your average employees just "wing it." Without the emotional engagement, these employees have already checked out, doing as much or as little as necessary to get through their day. Meanwhile, your customers, with no clear processes evident to get things done, don't know where to turn.

. . . Or Too Much

But ironically, too much process within a company can produce exactly the same results as too little. With a sea of process and technology to wade through, an ever-increasing framework designed to accommodate "any customer scenario," it becomes its own obstacle. There are inevitably situations that are, in fact, not accommodated, leaving a handcuffed employee with no flexibility to serve the customer's actual issue. And that's often where companies end up: Over time, as the company grows, it continues to add process for internal purposes, but without thought to the greater experience. The result is frustrated employees and angry customers.

Good Intentions Do Not Equal Good Process

Sometimes a process is created for all the right reasons but it's flawed in its execution, resulting in frustration for your customers. Here's an example: One morning I cut myself shaving while using a disposable razor one too many times. This was not the first time this had happened, and I was sick of it. So I decided to splurge and get myself a quality electric razor. No more cuts! No more shaving cream! It wasn't what you'd call "scoring the winning touchdown" exciting, but I looked forward to the purchase and subsequent painless, convenient shaving experiences to come and headed to that most American of struggling retailers—Sears.

It took a while to find what I was looking for, but eventually I came upon a large free-standing glass case with a vast array of electric razors. The case was locked, so I wandered around trying to locate an employee who might be able to open it for me. At first I was unsuccessful, but then I saw a number of employees back near the case. In fact, there was a small crowd standing next to the display; it appeared to be the floor's entire staff, all listening to the manager. Surely someone here had a key for the display!

But these employees were in the midst of what appeared to be a daily floor meeting—whose theme, ironically enough, seemed to be "the customer experience." I even heard the manager tell the younger staff members to be empathetic, to be good listeners, and to "focus on the customer's needs." Excellent! The only problem was that I needed some help and, although there was a small army of employees standing literally inches from the case that held the product I wanted to purchase, they were all "engaged" in a meeting discussing how to better serve people like, well, me. I looked across the store floor and noticed a few other customers standing idly near cash registers, eyes searching for an available employee, unbought merchandise in hand. The meeting continued and I eventually lost hope, finally wandering out to the parking lot, defeated.

The lesson here is that clearly process—well-intentioned or not—can have a negative impact on customer experience, and subsequently, on customer behavior as well as a positive one. The floor meeting was, by all appearances, a regular occurrence and was clearly geared on the right thing—improving experience for the Sears retail customer. The company was showing a commitment by creating a process of regular communication and feedback to employees from store managers. The idea was right; the execution was flawed. Think about your company's many touchpoints with customers. Surely, you can identify, without too much trouble, at least one process that is intended to make life easier for customers, but in fact does just the opposite. Process is a necessary evil, but it must be understood and actively managed—especially those processes that impact the customer experience.

The Danger of Groupthink— Process for Process's Sake

One of the causes of faulty customer processes within your company may be a type of inertia: a process that is in place, and has been in place for quite a while, but no one remembers just who created it, or when. Eventually, no one considers what impact, good or bad, the process is causing. And if someone takes a moment to consider the process, he or she doesn't do anything about it. This is an effect created, in part, by an aspect of human nature called "Groupthink."

Groupthink was an idea developed in Texas in the 1970s by social psychologist Irving Janis. The root of the idea occurred to him after he and his family made a decision to take a two-hour drive in their un-air-conditioned sedan on a hot, humid day for something to eat. After getting back home, each member of the group realized that he or she, in fact, had not wanted to travel into the city, but just went along with the rest of the group. Janis began to explore this phenomenon and developed the Groupthink theory.

Groupthink describes how a group makes a flawed decision (or, as is often the case, no decision at all) based on certain group pressures. There are several symptoms of Groupthink, among them self-censorship, where doubts and deviations from the group's consensus prevent a member from expressing an opinion; illusions of unanimity, where silence is perceived as assent; and "mindguards," self-appointed team members who shield the group from dissenting information. No doubt many people don't ever realize they are engaging in this type of behavior. The irrational subconscious of team members is pushing for behavior that is geared toward survival (not "rocking the boat," avoiding confrontation).

Groupthink applies to situations where innovative new solutions are suppressed by the strong group dynamic. It also refers to the inability of a group to change an existing situation. For instance, think of a large meeting you've attended where you could see there was an existing problem with a process, a problem that seemed to you as obvious, and yet no one stepped up to raise the issue or problem—no one, including you. Why is that? It's Groupthink at work, and it happens every day in companies everywhere.

When considered within the business world, Groupthink is a dynamic that can prevent people in a company from taking a fresh look at processes that might be obsolete or unworkable. Surely, you can see some examples of Groupthink within your company—processes that were there when you started that are never really discussed.

While Groupthink surely exists in some way or another in every company, there are ways to limit its impact. One is to instill the discipline within your company culture to allow people to ask the question, "Is this process the result of Groupthink?" Only by first acknowledging that this dynamic exists in any group setting, and then by encouraging employees to raise the issue, will you be able to give employees the permission to move beyond Groupthink and give voice to real issues. Another more specific step, which I describe in the next section, is to map out the customer experience so that you can take a fresh look at and improve your customer processes.

Developing a Customer Experience Process Map

We can all agree, I think, that most companies contain processes that aren't doing customers any favors. These processes, some purposeful and some perhaps inadvertent, are peppered throughout the typical customer experience. Your challenge is to uncover them so that you can determine which help the customer, which get in the way, and how to fix them when necessary.

One way we do this with our clients at Vox is by creating what we call a "Customer Experience Process Map." It's an exercise you can do yourself—with a little help from your internal departments and valuable frontline employees—that will get you a long way down the road to improving your processes in order to dramatically enhance the customer experience. The goal is to gain a better understanding of just what the customer experience looks like and to identify all the key processes that might impact it for better or worse. You do this by graphically laying out what the overall customer experience looks like, and then by identifying the various moments of truth within that experience. Only then can you, in a systematic and pragmatic way, begin to improve your processes as they relate to the customer.

Here's how we approach developing a customer experience process map. We gather the key players from the different internal areas of the company who have some perspective regarding the processes that might impact the customer, as well as representatives from the frontline positions who have direct contact with the company's customers. Finally, if possible, we recruit a couple of "typical" (as defined by the company) customers to participate in the session.

We then create a process map template—basically a glorified timeline. Next, we slowly walk through (in the customer's shoes, of course) a typical customer lifetime. For instance, for a bank there would be "account opening," which might take place either in person in the branch, on the phone, or on the bank's website. Then we continue down the path with the customer, identifying each moment of truth (an occasion that helps define the company-customer relationship, creating customer perception, emotion, and possibly behavior) and each associated process (things like account statements, cross-sale offers, and order fulfillment).

The exercise itself provides tremendous inherent value to the attendees by creating a unique picture of the customer experience that's actionable. We've found that this is often the first time that people in the company have gone to the trouble of actually understanding, in a comprehensive way, the full range of the customer experience. The result is a customer experience map, which can be leveraged in discussions on customer experience throughout the company.

Once the client has completed the map, we can analyze the assorted interactions and moments of truth and their corresponding processes. We then can unpack each of these processes, looking at what the employee does, what forms are filled out, what technology the employee utilizes, etc. The result is a clearer picture of what both the employee and the customer must confront to get something done. From there, you can move to improving the process.

Using Technology and Process for a More Human Customer Experience

It's funny. Some of our clients, especially larger companies, have become mired in process. There are processes for everything from how to handle returns or rebates to what to say to a customer in almost every conceivable situation. These processes can get in the way of creating real, memorable experiences. A given process, over time, becomes a rigid structure, something that employees lean on and use as an excuse, and also something that customers don't benefit from, but rather must suffer through, and even must develop their own strategies to contend with. Consider what we discussed in Chapter 9 regarding customer contact centers. Customers cringe when facing some of the processes they must contend with, such as a daunting interactive voice response system. In fact, the frustration has gotten so high that consumers can find strategies offered up online for beating the system, and getting around the IVR, such as hitting "1" multiple times or yelling "representative" to bypass the menus. It's a process that's supposedly designed for the customer, and yet often it appears to be developed with a focus on company efficiency, not customer service.

Some of our clients, on the other hand, barely have a process to stand on (forgive the mixed metaphor). They feel, and perhaps rightfully so, that their customers appreciate the human touch and that their employees care about delivering a high level of empathetic service. In a way, that's a great philosophy, but it's flawed. We worked with a bank client to help identify customer experience issues. When we pushed on the level of process concerning the customer experience, whether that involved the company's website, the way incoming phone calls were handled, or the method for creating and sending out customer communications, the inquiry was met by either a blank stare or a shrug and dismissive nod. "We do what's right for the customer," is the common refrain in those situations. Or "we're still a relatively small company. We don't need lots of processes."

But that's simply wrong. It doesn't matter how large or small your company is. You need to consciously build processes that, at the very least, provide a sort of safety net for your customers. Create processes to prevent a customer from feeling neglected or forgotten. Processes, when designed correctly, add to the customer experience. These days, especially, you have an opportunity to leverage technology tools to develop processes that serve the customer without requiring time or internal resources.

Here's an example of what I mean: Whether you have a large or small customer base, there are moments within the customer lifetime in which each customer may be more or less prone to purchase additional products or services from your company. Businesses that rely on renewal or subscription models are particularly sensitive (or should be) to these moments in the customer relationship. It makes sense to use technology and build a process to ensure your company is communicating regularly with customers as the date for renewal draws near, for instance. This could include a series of email communications (if that's what your customers prefer). It's critical that these communications go out automatically, without relying on human intervention.

But it's more than automating something. Today you can use technology to better understand the circumstances of each customer, to customize the delivery of your product or service without requiring more time from your employees, and do this while making the customer experience more human. In other words, use systems and processes and technology to raise the bar on personal customer experience and make heroes out of your frontline employees.

The Process to Keep Every New Customer: Onboarding

Frankly, it doesn't matter to me what industry you are in (although I'm sure it does to you). Regardless of the type of company, there are some universal truths regarding how you establish customer relationships. Whether you provide a service or product, and whether it's to consumers or business clients, you need to create a process that's intended specifically to bring the customer into the fold and to generate positive emotions for the customer about his or her association with your company.

Why is this so important? Here's one reason: Research in the banking industry showed that, within the first six months of the customer relationship, a customer is most likely to either purchase additional products or to leave.[1] Think about the implications of this: Your newer customers are trusting you and trying to feel good about associating with your company, but they are also insecure and looking for any indication, one way or another, as to just how you, the company, will likely treat them. If a customer feels ignored in the early stages of the relationship, he or she will look for some way to escape. If, on the other hand, the customer feels taken care of and senses a strong commitment from the company to the relationship, there is a golden opportunity to lock that customer in for the long haul.

It's up to you to determine the fate of your new customers. You do this by creating an *onboarding* process. What do I mean by onboarding? It's really a simple concept. Develop a process that ensures that each new customer moves through a series of steps that cumulatively and purposefully build a positive perception in the mind of the customer. In other words, systematically welcome and engage the customer over the first days, weeks, or months of the relationship. You don't need a sophisticated system to start down this road. By implementing some simple processes, you can begin to strengthen the relationship when it's at its most vulnerable. Simply by setting up a three- or four-step process, you can significantly improve your customer retention.

An onboarding process can include both automatic aspects (such as, for instance, a welcome letter or package that is sent at a predetermined time after a sale) and human interaction, such as a scheduled contact with a new customer and employee, like a phone call or email. Again, this can begin as simple stuff. Once you initiate an onboarding process, you can test it and add sophistication as your capabilities increase.

The Key to Irrational Customer Processes: Empowerment

You have a chance, if you approach it the right way, to eliminate processes that inhibit the customer experience and to improve or create processes that enhance it. You and your employees should look at process not as obstacle but as enabler. A well-thought-out, well-executed customer process doesn't handcuff good employees; rather, it empowers them to be heroes in the eyes of the customer. This brings me to an overall recommendation: When considering process, always evaluate how to create it in a way that empowers your frontline employees, that gives employees the freedom to truly wow the customer.

Ritz-Carlton Hotels provides a world-class illustration of how to approach employee accountability and empowerment as part of your customer service process. The chain places a high priority on the training of its employees and the overall excellence of its customer service. Part of that training is focused on instilling a high level of accountability in its frontline employees (for instance, one of the customer service tenets is that an employee "owns" a customer issue until it is resolved; no "passing the buck" allowed). Along with that accountability, the company provides an incredible level of empowerment to its front desk staff: specifically, the freedom to spend up to $2,000 to resolve an issue for a customer. That's right, two grand. When I mention this to business people, they are incredulous. "$2,000!"

But when you understand the company business model, it makes sense. The average lifetime value for a typical Ritz-Carlton customer is approximately $250,000. On the rare occasion when a desk employee spends a significant amount of money to appease a customer (and, no doubt, that's usually nothing close to $2,000), the company sees it as an investment, not an expense. It's easy to accept that cost when the lifetime value of a customer is many times that.

The point here is that any customer-focused process should include a healthy dose of flexibility for frontline employees. By combining the structure and tools of a well-thought-out process with the empowerment of engaged employees, your company is more likely to create memorable, positive customer experiences.

So . . . What Do I Do Now?

You need process. Your company needs process. And your customers need process. The trick is to create processes that effectively serve those different constituencies. Your customers are irrational and make decisions based on a variety of stimuli. They are heavily influenced not just by the communications and interactions you share with them, but by the processes that support those interactions. So, how do you create processes that help your cause with your customers and don't hinder their experience?

1. *Build Your Customer Experience Process Map.* You cannot begin to create or improve customer-impacting processes until you identify exactly what they are. Put an internal team together and develop your customer experience process map—a graphical representation of the customer experience, highlighting those moments of truth and their associated processes. Then analyze each process to determine if it's necessary and, if so, if it can be improved.

2. *Create an Onboarding Process.* Research shows that your newer customers are vulnerable. During the first few months of the relationship, they are more likely to purchase additional products from you, and conversely, more likely to leave than at any other time. You must build a process to nurture and develop a level of trust and emotional connection in the first weeks or months of the relationship. Customers are insecure and seek out emotional connections, which is an opportunity for you to establish a deeper relationship. Without a thoughtful onboarding process, you risk wasting the money you spent on customer acquisition, as well as the opportunity to make additional sales.

3. *Empower Your Frontline Employees.* Yes, you need processes, but you also need to build the flexibility necessary for your frontline employees to have the freedom to "do what's right" for your customers. You can empower through training and policies that allow your employees to use their own skills and sense of empathy to better serve your customers. By empowering your employees, you're also building trust with them, which leads to a higher level of engagement. And engaged employees exploit their empowerment eagerly, in ways that enhance the customer experience, and ultimately improve the financial performance of the company as well.

Chapter 12

Getting Started: Three Action Steps You Need to Take First

Action always generates inspiration. Inspiration seldom generates action.

Frank Tibolt

What to do? Where to start?

We've explored many aspects of customer experience throughout this book, analyzing just how your customers really think (hint: irrationally) and what implications that has for you as you attempt to improve the customer experience at your own company, and in turn your retention and profitability. And, as you have no doubt noticed, we have ended each chapter with a few action items to help you begin making progress toward understanding, attracting, and retaining your customers.

But that's not enough, is it? When I think of the many business books I've pored through, I know what often happens next . . . nothing. You read the book, nod affirmatively on occasion, agreeing with the insights or concepts espoused, and then you go back to your real job. So what I want to do for you is some cheerleading. Do something! This is too important an issue to be in passive agreement. It's up to you to get your company moving in the right direction toward understanding your irrational customers and driving the desired customer behavior.

I know there are a lot of tips in this book, and it's sometimes hard to know where to start, so I'm here to help! What follows are three action steps you can take to begin your journey toward an improved experience for your customers. These include some of the key pieces of advice that are found throughout the book, but are organized here in such a way as to get you moving in the right direction. If you follow these three steps, I'm confident that you will make substantial progress on your customer experience improvement efforts. So here they are:

> *Step One:* Create a "Customer Experience Scorecard."
> *Step Two:* Conduct your own "Customer Experience Audit."
> *Step Three:* Start small.

If you take these steps, in order, you'll soon be making a real impact within your company.

Step One: Create a Customer Experience Scorecard: Understand Your Numbers

One of the first concepts we discussed in this book was the idea that—given that you have irrational customers—"behavior is truth." Because your customers, indeed all of us, process emotions and make decisions largely in the irrational subconscious, they are not very good at accessing and articulating their true feelings regarding your products or services. Customers are also poor at predicting what they might think, or how they might act, in the future. The answer, therefore, is to focus not on what your customers say, but on what they do.

And the way to do that is through the numbers.

If you bought and read this book, you clearly see the value of improving the customer experience at your own company. But you might be confronted with some resistance in terms of expending time and resources toward real customer focus. Many businesses still don't see the connection between a better customer experience and a healthier bottom line, so it may be up to you to come up with ammunition—solid evidence and rationale that customer retention efforts are just as, if not more, important as customer acquisition efforts. In other words, remember the oft-used business phrase, "that which gets measured gets done."

Here's what you need to do: Create a "customer experience scorecard." A scorecard is simply a report that tracks several key metrics. It can be an electronic or paper report; something that is delivered to key management daily, weekly, or monthly; or a report that can be accessed in real time through a Web-based or internal system. The important thing is to determine just what you can begin tracking so you can gauge how the company is performing regarding its customer relationships and customer behavior.

The customer metrics you choose to track will be determined by several issues. First, what information is currently available to you? All companies are different regarding how they look at and track customers, but there are a few universal customer metrics. You should be able to get your hands on total revenue and total number of customers, for instance. Divide your total revenue by the number of customers, and you have average annual revenue per customer.

The other factor is determining just which numbers are the most important for your company. Which measurements, given your specific business model, tell you the most over the long term about the health of your customer experience and its bottom-line impact?

Let's build a quick example so you have a better sense of how to start your own customer experience scorecard. Say you are a service company, perhaps a plumbing company. You do commercial and residential work, so you have relationships with real estate developers, home builders, and homeowners. Because you are limited geographically to a service area that includes only a few adjacent towns, your success is dependent on repeat customers. For the most part, your commercial and new home construction jobs pay more than the typical residential, but the volume is higher (you think) on your residential jobs.

Given that scenario, what do you track? Here are a few possibilities. The most basic measurement (if we start with baby steps) is the total number of current customers, and following that, overall customer retention. It's surprising to me how many companies have no idea how many customers they have, and of those, how many they're holding onto each subsequent year. If those numbers aren't obvious already to everybody in the organization, make it a priority to change that situation.

There's also the issue of the average customer lifetime value. If you know the average revenue per customer per year, you can just go to our website, www.voxinc.com, and refer to the customer calculators to get your baseline on this (as well as to help you with other customer metrics). If you can look at your data and begin to segment your customer base, you'll be able to make more sophisticated decisions. In this instance, you might be able to tag your three types of customers—real estate developers, home builders, and homeowners—in a simple database.

Often, most of this data exists somewhere in your company already; you just might not be getting exposed to it. It's really a matter of reaching out to the folks who may "own" the information and setting up a simple way to share it. At first, that might mean asking them to send you the data at regular intervals, but eventually it's optimal if the information from the different areas automatically flows to one person or department who compiles it into one system.

The customer experience scorecard introduces a discipline that is lacking in many businesses—understanding the true impact of your customers on your bottom line. Once you've established which numbers are both relevant to tracking your performance as it relates to customers and overall customer behavior, you can create your scorecard and begin leveraging it to get people inside the company onboard the customer experience train.

It may seem daunting to determine just what to measure, and how. And I can't tell you exactly which metrics will make the most sense for your company. But the key is to start measuring your customers' behavior *any way you can*. What you'll find is that simply the act of starting to track behavior will help you to make a leap in your understanding of your customers, and that knowledge will give you additional leverage to convince others within the company of the importance of the customer experience.

Step Two: Conduct a Customer Experience Audit: Discover the Customer's Perspective

As Marshall Field said, your customers are your only profit center. Yet most companies spend very little time or energy trying to understand of all the different experiences a customer perceives as he or she interacts with your company. Think about your customers and all the touchpoints (or "moments of truth") over the course of a customer lifetime with your business. Do you really understand what the customer is encountering at each interaction? Most businesses would say no.

That is why one of the first steps you should take in order to really understand what your customers are going through is to conduct a customer experience audit. A customer experience audit is really an extension of a concept we've mentioned a few times throughout the book: to "walk in your customer's shoes." The idea is to take the empathetic approach to your customers to an extreme of sorts. You must look over the customer experience as a whole to understand the full spectrum and variety of interactions, and then "walk in the customer's shoes" through each of these moments of truth and analyze the quality of each.

A customer experience audit is something that we do for our clients at Vox, although we call it a "Customerspective Audit," but you can do it yourself. Through this process, you can gain a new level of insight into where you are succeeding and where you are failing with your customers.

Let's break down the steps of a customer experience audit. First, you need to identify the scope of your audit. In other words, you've got to identify all the different experiences a customer might have with your company. You can start with something we discussed in Chapter 11—creating a customer experience process map. As I mentioned then, the customer experience process map is simply a timeline showing a typical customer lifetime, with every probable interaction identified. (I say "probable" because it's very easy to get overwhelmed with all the "possible" interactions between customer and company. Keep it simple to start.)

Using the customer experience process map, you can then walk through each of those interactions from the customer's perspective. Does this sound simplistic? It is! Does it seem like something every company should already be doing? It is! But just because it's obvious and easy doesn't mean most companies take the time to do it. It's enlightening to get a customer perspective on your services, products, and communications. Just because nobody at your company has bothered to do this before should not stop you from doing it now! This is not something to casually assign to others. You will understand the issues confronting your customers only if you confront the customer experience yourself, or at least have direct involvement with the effort and findings.

To actually walk through these experiences might take a little imagination, but you will learn a tremendous amount in a short period of time. Here are some examples of things you can start to take a look at. If you have statements, bills, or other basic customer communications, take the time to gather them, understand exactly when they are being sent (and why), and read them from a customer perspective. Are they written using language that's common within the company or industry, but not to customers (a common problem)? Do they make sense? Are they relevant to the relationship between the customer and your company? Do they actually add value? What about incoming calls from clients or customers? One thing we've noticed is that companies rarely bother to listen to how their own phone system works. Sometimes the "message-on-hold" content (what you hear while waiting on hold) doesn't work properly, is old, is irritating, or doesn't do anything to make the customer feel appreciated or welcome.

You can also observe customers' behavior in any form or forum possible, while they are using your products, navigating through your website, shopping in your retail location, or eating in your restaurant. Some of your methods can be quantifiable, and others can be anecdotal. Any information you glean regarding the current customer experience can be helpful. Don't discount what you learn simply because it's not scientifically gathered or analyzed.

Finally, talk to a few customers. Just remember to take what they say with a grain of salt, because they can't tell you what's in their irrational subconscious, which ultimately creates emotions and drives their behavior. Still, you can glean valuable insight by asking behavior-based questions such as "When did you receive a welcome letter?" or "Did one of our employees call you when we had promised?"

The point here is that this isn't rocket science. It doesn't take any specific set of skills, beyond the ability to imagine oneself as a customer, to walk through these different experiences. Take the trouble and see just what you learn. You'll be amazed.

Step Three: Start Small: The Secret Is *Incremental* Improvement

There is an interesting (and sometimes discouraging) phenomenon we've seen play itself out at a number of companies. There are brilliant executives who understand the importance that the role of customer experience plays in a company's overall financial performance. They see the logic of improving retention, cross sales, and referrals, and the connection to lower acquisition costs and greater profitability. But often these customer advocates trip up on their very first step. They make a grand statement or gesture of some sort, trying to accomplish something major regarding a company commitment to customer experience, but they do it prematurely, before a compelling case for focusing on and improving customer experience has really been made.

It almost never works. Especially in larger companies, different aspects of the customer experience reside in different parts of the company. And the folks managing those different areas may not see the need to jump on the customer experience bandwagon. This is true even if those championing the efforts are on the senior management team.

The result is that there is a big splash of some sort, some over-the-top clarion call for a company-wide focus on customer experience, but because actual action or improvement—of a magnitude to match the decibel level—just isn't possible for a plethora of reasons (the sheer inertia within the company, as well as conflicting motivations for management in the various business units of a company), any customer-focused initiative can quickly lose steam.

The answer to this is basic: To start improving the customer experience, try to hit singles, not home runs. If you overreach, you could swamp your entire effort. Better to pick goals—based on what you've found out through both your customer experience scorecard and your customer experience audit—that you know are attainable without requiring the involvement of a large number of other people or departments within your organization.

It's only by creating some initial successes that you can begin to engage others within the company. If people see evidence that the improvements actually happen, and that those efforts have some positive impact on department or company performance, a customer focus becomes a much easier sell.

Where can you start? How do you pick an attainable customer experience goal? Look for something that's a real problem, a situation that you can improve without requiring unreasonable internal or external resources. And be sure you can demonstrate through some metric that the situation has been improved.

For example, we once worked with an insurance company to help improve the customer perception of its claims process. The small army of claims representatives throughout the country dealt with customers largely through a network of letters generated through a system at the home office. To accommodate an increasing array of situations, the number of letters had grown to over 400. It was entirely up to the claims representative to determine which letter to send, and when to send it, depending on the situation. We reviewed all the letters (i.e., read them from a customer's perspective). Many of them were almost incomprehensible. Some were harsh in tone, even to the company's customers.

This was a project that only needed to involve the claims department with a little help from the legal area. We weren't setting unreasonable expectations, so the risks were low. By simply reviewing all the letters, we concluded that there were a number of them that were intended for similar situations; since nobody was controlling the overall communications, letters were being randomly created over time. So our first step was to simply eliminate dozens of letters that were no longer necessary. Then we rewrote the remaining letters so that they were more accessible, more human in tone, and showed some empathy for the customer's situation.

An insurance claim is perhaps one of the most emotional of any customer experience. If a customer feels insulted, ignored, or slighted (all memorable emotions that can drive customer behavior), he or she is more likely to avoid a quick settlement, which costs the company more money, not to mention the negative impact on retention. That may not seem like rational behavior from your customers but, as we've seen, we cannot expect our customers to act in a completely rational way.

Through a relatively inexpensive process of reviewing, eliminating, and rewriting of claims letters, we were able to effect positive changes in the customer experience, and this could be tracked in a number of ways, including average time to settlement.

Pick something that is broken, that you have the capability to improve, and then track the results. Then move on to the next customer experience issue. By incrementally improving aspects of the customer experience that you have some control or influence over, you will achieve success, gain additional traction within your organization, and move on to the next, larger challenge.

If there's a message you should take from this book, it's this: Your customers are irrational in how they interact with the world, but they act based on, for the most part, the same things you do—a deep emotional need to feel a sense of belonging, a sense that they are valued, that you actually care. Stop looking at your customer issues rationally. Your customers don't. Companies that recognize this, and that execute their business models accordingly, are the leaders in the marketplace. If you are not part of one of those companies, you can begin today to show your organization the way toward the customer experience light. Observe and measure how your customers behave. Then begin to incrementally improve each aspect of the customer experience.

Don't wait! Start right now!

Notes

Chapter 1

1. Varva, Terry, *How to Win Back Lost Customers,* Direct Marketing to Business Report (October 1, 1995), p. 7.

2. Cope, Debra, "In Search of the Loyal Customer," *Community Banker* (March 1, 2006).

3. Alsever, Jennifer, *Wireless Price War to Benefit Cell-Phone Addicts,* msnbc.com (February 28, 2008).

4. Cope, op. cit.

5. Murphy, Emmet, & Murphy, Mark, *Leading on the Edge of Chaos* (Upper Saddle River, NJ: Prentice Hall, 2002), p. 30.

Chapter 2

1. Wilson, Timothy, *Strangers to Ourselves* (Cambridge, MA: Harvard University Press, 2002).

2. Zaltman, Gerald, *How Customers Think* (Cambridge, MA: Harvard Business School Press, 2003).

3. Described in Dijksterhuis, Ap, Bos, Maarten W., Nordgren, Loran F., & van Baaren, Rick B., "On Making the Right Choice: The Deliberation Without Attention Effect," *Science, 311* (February 17, 2006), 1005–1007.

4. Damasio, Antonio, *Descartes' Error* (New York: Harper Perennial, 1995).

5. Du Plessis, Erik, *The Advertised Mind* (Sterling, VA: MillwardBrown, 2005).

6. Linden, David, *The Accidental Mind* (Cambridge, MA: Belknap Press, 2007).

Chapter 3

1. *2008 American Customer Satisfaction Index*, University of Michigan.

2. Denove, Chris, & Power, James D. IV, *Satisfaction: How Every Great Company Listens to the Voice of the Customer* (Edmonton, AB: Portfolio Hardcover, 2006).

3. Freiberg, Kevin, & Freiberg, Jackie, *Nuts: Southwest Airlines' Crazy Recipe for Business and Personal Success* (New York: Random House, 1998).

Chapter 4

1. Vaglio, Wick, *Creating a Competitive Advantage: Using Differentiation as the Key to Small Business Acquisition*. ABA Conference Marketing Notes (September 7, 2007).

2. Reichheld, Frederick, & Teal, Thomas, *The Loyalty Effect: The Hidden Force Behind Growth, Profits, and Lasting Value* (Boston: Harvard Business School Press, 1996).

3. Wilson, Timothy, *Strangers to Ourselves* (Cambridge, MA: Harvard University Press, 2002), p. 207.

4. Ibid.

5. Underhill, Paco, *Why We Buy: The Science of Shopping* (New York: Simon & Schuster, 1999).

Chapter 5

1. Gladwell, Malcolm, *Blink* (New York: Little Brown and Company, 2005).

2. Carey, Benedict, "Who's Minding the Mind?" *New York Times* (July 21, 2007).

3. Gigerenzer, Gerd, *Gut Feelings: The Intelligence of the Unconscious* (New York: Viking, 2007), p. 99.

Chapter 6

1. Klein, Gary, *Sources of Power* (Cambridge, MA: MIT Press, 1998).

2. Wilson, Timothy, *Strangers to Ourselves* (Cambridge, MA: Harvard University Press, 2002), p. 171.

3. Maister, David, *The Trusted Advisor* (New York: Free Press, 2000).

4. Gigerenzer, Gerd, *Gut Feelings: The Intelligence of the Unconscious* (New York: Viking, 2007).

Chapter 7

1. Reeves, Byron, & Nass, Clifford, *The Media Equation: How People Treat Computers, Television, and New Media Like Real People and Places* (New York: Cambridge University Press, 1996).

Chapter 8

1. Carey, Benedict, "This Is Your Life (and How You Tell It)," *New York Times* (May 22, 2007).

Chapter 9

1. Norman, Donald, *Emotional Design* (New York: Basic Books, 2004).

2. DiSalvo, Carl, & Gemperie, Francine, *From Seduction to Fulfillment: The Use of Anthropomorphic Form in Design* (Pittsburgh, PA: Carnegie Mellon University, 2003).

3. Heller, Steven, "Breakthrough: Scientists Find Emotions Influence Designs," *Voice: AIGA Journal of Design* (February 17, 2004).

4. Reinhardt, Andy, "Steve Jobs: 'There's Sanity Returning,'" *Business Week* (May 25, 1998).

5. Surowiecki, Jame, "Feature Presentation," The Financial Page, *The New Yorker* (May 28, 2007).

Chapter 10

1. Meyer, Danny, *Setting the Table* (New York: HarperCollins, 2006).

2. Hess, Edward, *The Road to Organic Growth* (New York: McGraw Hill, 2007), p. 115.

Chapter 11

1. Wachtel, Christopher, "All Aboard," *ABA Bank Marketing* (December 2007), p. 17.

Index

About the Author

William Cusick is CEO and Founder of Vox, Inc., a successful Customer Experience consulting firm in Chicago. Mr. Cusick started Vox in 1997. The company helps clients to increase profitability and customer retention by strategically improving the customer experience. Vox has worked with Fortune 500 companies, including Allstate Insurance, Zurich North America, CNA, 21st Century Insurance, and Commerce Clearing House, as well as many smaller companies.

Mr. Cusick worked for eleven years at Allstate Insurance, where he ran a variety of communications, advertising, and branding programs. While leading the Customer Communications area, he attended law school at night, graduated with honors, wrote for the law review, and passed the Illinois bar exam.

As CEO and founder of Vox, Mr. Cusick has continued to address a vast number of client needs in a variety of industries. He has been exploring questions that surround the customer experience for his entire professional career (over twenty years).

Mr. Cusick lives in a (relatively) draft-free Victorian in Oak Park, Illinois, with his wife, three children, and two dogs.